HOUS

European Union Committee

7th Report of Session 2007–08

The Future of the Common Agricultural Policy

Volume I: Report

Ordered to be printed 26 February 2008 and published 6 March 2008

Published by the Authority of the House of Lords

London : The Stationery Office Limited

£14.50

HL Paper 54–I

The European Union Committee

The European Union Committee is appointed by the House of Lords "to consider European Union documents and other matters relating to the European Union". The Committee has seven Sub-Committees which are:

Economic and Financial Affairs, and International Trade (Sub-Committee A)
Internal Market (Sub-Committee B)
Foreign Affairs, Defence and Development Policy (Sub-Committee C)
Environment and Agriculture (Sub-Committee D)
Law and Institutions (Sub-Committee E)
Home Affairs (Sub-Committee F)
Social and Consumer Affairs (Sub-Committee G)

Our Membership

The Members of the European Union Committee are:

Lord Blackwell
Baroness Cohen of Pimlico
Lord Dykes
Lord Freeman
Lord Grenfell (Chairman)
Lord Harrison
Baroness Howarth of Breckland
Lord Jopling
Lord Kerr of Kinlochard
Lord Maclennan of Rogart

Lord Mance
Lord Plumb
Lord Powell of Bayswater
Lord Roper
Lord Sewel
Baroness Symons of Vernham Dean
Lord Tomlinson
Lord Wade of Chorlton
Lord Wright of Richmond

The Members of Sub-Committee D (Environment and Agriculture) who participated in this inquiry are:

Earl of Arran
Lord Bach (up to 10 November 2007)
Lord Brooke of Alverthorpe
Viscount Brookeborough
Lord Cameron of Dillington
Earl of Dundee
Lord Greaves
Baroness Jones of Whitchurch

Baroness Miller of Chilthorne Domer (up to 9 November 2007)
Lord Moynihan (up to 10 November 2007)
Lord Palmer
Lord Plumb
Lord Sewel (Chairman)
Baroness Sharp of Guildford
Viscount Ullswater

Information about the Committee

The reports and evidence of the Committee are published by and available from The Stationery Office. For information freely available on the web, our homepage is:
http://www.parliament.uk/parliamentary_committees/lords_eu_select_committee.cfm
There you will find many of our publications, along with press notices, details of membership and forthcoming meetings, and other information about the ongoing work of the Committee and its Sub-Committees, each of which has its own homepage.

General Information

General information about the House of Lords and its Committees, including guidance to witnesses, details of current inquiries and forthcoming meetings is on the internet at
http://www.parliament.uk/about_lords/about_lords.cfm

Contacts for the European Union Committee

Contact details for individual Sub-Committees are given on the website.
General correspondence should be addressed to the Clerk of the European Union Committee, Committee Office, House of Lords, London, SW1A OPW
The telephone number for general enquiries is 020 7219 5791.
The Committee's email address is euclords@parliament.uk

CONTENTS

NOTE: References in the text of the report are as follows:
(Q) refers to a question in oral evidence
(p) refers to a page of written evidence
(Para.) refers to a paragraph of written evidence

The evidence received in the course of this inquiry is published in Volume II (HL Paper 54-II)

FOREWORD—What this Report is about

The 2003 reform of the Common Agricultural Policy marked the culmination of a gradual reorientation of EU farm subsidies from product support to direct income support. A mid-term "Health Check" of this reform is now underway, exploring what further adjustments may be required for the period 2009 to 2013. The initiative is a stepping-stone ahead of the 2008/09 Budget Review, which will examine all aspects of EU expenditure—including spending on the CAP, which has traditionally been the largest single item of budget expenditure.

In this report, we look ahead at what the long-term goals of the Common Agricultural Policy should be, before examining whether the preliminary reform proposals set out in the European Commission's "Health Check" Communication would steer policy in the right direction. We then turn to the medium- and long-term future of the instruments through which the CAP is delivered, exploring how these should be adapted for the period after 2013, when the current financial settlement expires.

We conclude that—with a limited number of exceptions—the Commission's proposals for short-term adjustments to the CAP merit support. However, we are not convinced of the long-term justification for maintaining direct subsidy payments in their present form. We consequently advocate a phased reduction in direct payments over the course of the next financial period beginning in 2014. In order to facilitate an orderly transition, we recommend that a significant proportion of the funds released should remain earmarked for the CAP, but be spent on the rural development element of the policy rather than on farm subsidies. We do not envisage a Common Rural Policy, but rather an EU-level framework defining admissible uses for EU rural development funds, ruling out measures that might lead to distortions in the Single Market for agricultural commodities.

In the course of our report, we also address the challenges and opportunities that lie ahead for the EU agriculture industry. We note that the sector is a significant contributor to climate change, while at the same time being particularly vulnerable to its effects. Climate change may nevertheless present a business opportunity for the industry, which is uniquely placed to deliver environmental services.

We observe that soaring global demand for many agricultural commodities has allowed some sectors of the European farming industry to prosper, while others are grappling with rising input prices and stagnant or falling output prices. Were supply shortages to ensue in future, we expect that food scarcity would be a function of income rather than of production capacity. In our view, those most at risk are therefore consumers on low incomes in the developing world.

We strongly support further trade liberalization in the agriculture sector, but note that if direct payments are withdrawn and import tariffs reduced—as the UK Government advocates—then the production standards that EU producers of agricultural goods are obliged to meet should be re-examined.

The Future of the Common Agricultural Policy

CHAPTER 1: INTRODUCTION AND FACTUAL BACKGROUND

Purpose and Scope of this Inquiry, Structure of this Report

1. The Committee's inquiry has been motivated by two forthcoming EU initiatives. The first is the decision to subject the 2003 reform[1] of the CAP to a "Health Check" in 2008. The second initiative is the Budget Review to be undertaken by the European Commission in 2008/09. The Review is being carried out in response to a request made by the European Council in December 2005, when political agreement on the current 2007–2013 Financial Perspective was reached (Council Document 15915/05). One of the specific elements of EU spending to be addressed in the Review is the CAP.

2. The European Commissioner for Agriculture and Rural Development, Mariann Fischer Boel, has described these two initiatives as "one vision, two steps", suggesting that an "adjustment" of current arrangements will take place through the 2008 Health Check, while the Budget Review will address the CAP's future post-2013.

3. The purpose of the Committee's inquiry was to take stock of the 2003 CAP reform, and to consider whether further reform may be required in both the short and long term. This report is intended to respond to the Commission's Communication on the Health Check (published on November 20 2007), and to feed into the debate over the longer-term direction of the CAP in anticipation of the Budget Review.

4. In the course of our inquiry, we came to the conclusion that it would be essential to look ahead at what the long-term goals of the Common Agricultural Policy should be before attempting to evaluate whether the proposals contained in the Commission's Communication on the Health Check are taking policy in the right direction. Once the factual background to this inquiry has been set out, our report therefore considers what the long-term goals of the CAP should be, before returning to the instruments that may be used to deliver them, and how these might be adapted in the short and longer term.

5. The inquiry that led to this report was carried out by EU Sub-Committee D, whose Members are listed in Appendix 1. We received written evidence and heard oral evidence from a wide range of witnesses, who are listed in Appendix 2. We are grateful to them all for their contributions. We would also like to thank those who facilitated our visits to Brussels and Edinburgh. We are particularly indebted to Sir John Marsh, our Specialist Adviser on this inquiry. We make this report to the House for debate.

Introducing the CAP post-2003

6. The CAP reforms agreed in 2003 represent a radical shift in the EU's agricultural policy. Historically, the CAP has supported farmers' incomes

---

[1] Council Regulation 1782/2003 of 29 September 2003 and its implementing regulations. This Committee published a report on the external implications of this mid-term review of the CAP on March 27 2003.

and stimulated production through guaranteed product prices. By the 1980s, however, this policy had not only eliminated post-war food shortages but also resulted in costly surpluses of major agricultural commodities. The MacSharry reform of 1992 began to reduce the level of support prices for a number of commodities, in exchange for direct payments to farmers to compensate them for the resulting loss of income. The Agenda 2000 reform agreed in 1999 further reduced support prices, and introduced an integrated rural development policy intended to form a 'second pillar' of the CAP. The mid-term review of the Agenda 2000 agreement resulted in the 2003 CAP reform, which marks the culmination of a gradual shift in farm support from product support to direct income support.

7.   Today, the CAP thus rests on two "pillars": Pillar I, out of which direct payments to farmers and market management measures are funded, and Pillar II, which supports rural development and environmental programmes.

TABLE 1

CAP Expenditure over the 2007–2013 Financial Perspective

Figures in billions of euros, based on 2004 prices	Total 2007–2013
Pillar I—Direct Payments and Market Support	293, 105
Pillar II—Rural Development	69, 750

Pillar I

8.   The main element of the 2003 Fischler reform—as with the 1992 reform, named after the Commissioner who proposed it—is the "decoupling" of subsidies from production in most sectors. All previous production-linked payments were bundled into a Single Farm Payment, to be paid to farmers on the basis of payments received during a reference period (historical basis) or the number of eligible hectares farmed during a reference period (area basis). To be eligible to receive Single Farm Payments, farmers are obliged to meet certain public, animal and plant health standards, to respect certain environmental and animal welfare standards, and to keep their land in good agricultural and environmental condition (GAEC). This element of conditionality associated with Single Farm Payments is known as cross-compliance. It has been presented as the public benefit delivered in return for Single Farm Payments.

BOX 1

What is cross-compliance?

In order to be eligible to receive their full Single Farm Payment, farmers are required to meet a number of Statutory Management Requirements (SMRs) and to maintain their land in good agricultural and environmental condition (GAEC).

Statutory Management Requirements derive from the provisions of existing EU legislation on environmental, public, animal and plant health and animal welfare. By 2007, aspects of 19 EU Directives or Regulations had been included in the list of SMRs.

Farmers must also abide by standards set in each Member State with respect to the maintenance of land in good agricultural and environmental condition. Each government establishes its own definition of GAEC by setting requirements under a number of headings (e.g. soil management) that were agreed by all Member States as part of the 2003 CAP reform.

Failure by farmers to respect one or both of these elements of cross compliance can result in deductions from, or complete cancellation of, Single Farm Payments.

9. The decoupling of payments from production does not extend to all sectors. The 2003 agreement allows Member States to maintain some specific production-related direct aid where this is considered necessary to secure a minimum level of productive activity and environmental benefits. Most of the EU-15[2] thus maintain coupled or partially coupled payments in some sectors. Under Article 69 of the 2003 Regulation[3] introducing the reform, Member States were also given the option of retaining up to 10 per cent of their National Envelope[4] for a particular sector to support agricultural activities that are important for the environment or for improving the quality and marketing of agricultural products. A smaller proportion of Member States have taken advantage of this provision, but in Scotland, for example, it has been used to provide support for the Scottish Beef Calf Scheme.

10. The 2003 reform placed greater emphasis on modulation—the mechanism whereby funds earmarked for direct payments to farmers under Pillar I can be diverted to fund measures under Pillar II. The Agenda 2000 reform already offered Member States the option to apply modulation on a voluntary basis, but few chose to do so. The 2003 reform introduced compulsory rates of modulation, intended to fund additional rural development measures. Member States can, however, continue to apply additional, voluntary modulation. Only the UK and Portugal have chosen to take advantage of this option.

BOX 2

What is modulation?

The term "modulation" is used to describe the transfer of funds from direct subsidy payments under Pillar I of the CAP to rural development expenditure under Pillar II of the CAP. It is a mechanism used to shift financial resources across otherwise separate budget lines.

Compulsory modulation was applied to all but the smallest farms in the EU-15 at a rate of 3 per cent in 2005, rising to 4 per cent in 2006 and 5 per cent in 2007. It is currently due to continue at 5 per cent until 2012, but the rate may be raised as part of the Health Check.

Member States or regions can opt for additional, "voluntary" modulation, reducing spending on direct payments by a maximum of 20 per cent. Under a compromise reached by the Council in March 2007, only the UK and Portugal will continue to make use of this option.[5]

At least 80 per cent of funds from compulsory modulation are retained in the Member State where they were raised. By contrast, funds from voluntary modulation are retained in their entirety in the Member State where they were generated.

11. Although the decoupling of subsidies was designed to encourage farmers to produce in response to market demand, a series of market management instruments have been retained. These include production quotas (e.g. for milk), set-aside (whereby farmers must leave a proportion of their arable land fallow or use it for non-agricultural purposes) and export refunds, as well as intervention storage. These instruments were originally introduced in order to control the supply of agricultural commodities by reducing production and in order to clear surpluses.

---

[2] Those Member States who joined the EU prior to 2004. For practice in the new Member States—those that have joined since 2004—see Box 4.

[3] Council Regulation No. 1782/2003 EC

[4] The term 'National Envelope' is used to refer to a funding allocation that Member States are given flexibility to distribute according to their own priorities.

[5] See Council Regulation 378/2007.

Pillar II

12. Rural development policy has emerged in a piecemeal way, as a result of successive reforms of the CAP. In 2005, however, existing programmes and budget lines were pulled together into a single funding and programming instrument known as the European Agricultural Fund for Rural Development (EAFRD). The fund supports projects across three 'axes': Axis 1 covers measures designed to improve the competitiveness of the farming and forestry industry, Axis 2 covers environmental and land-management schemes, while Axis 3 covers initiatives aimed at improving quality of life and the diversification of the rural economy. A fourth, separate, element of the fund is reserved for LEADER[6] initiatives, whereby local action groups in rural areas can secure funding for local development projects.

13. Rural development policy under the EAFRD is implemented through national strategy plans prepared by each Member State on the basis of domestic priorities. These plans must be approved by the Commission, and are subsequently delivered through rural development programmes in each member state. In drawing up their plans, member states must respect certain minimum spending requirements in each of the four categories. Once plans are approved, spending must be co-financed according to fixed percentages, meaning that Member States must contribute national resources in addition to the funds provided by the EU.

BOX 3

The EAFRD

Council Regulation 1698/2005 introduced a single instrument to finance rural development policy under Pillar II of the CAP from 2007: the European Agricultural Fund for Rural Development (EAFRD).

The Fund provides financial support for actions under three headings or "axes", with minimum spending requirements attached to each, to ensure that Member States spend their allocated funds across all three objectives. Rules on co-financing rates (determining the relative financial contribution of the EU and the Member State) also apply.

Axis 1 of the Fund—on which a minimum of 15 per cent of allocated funds must be spent—aims to support measures designed to improve the competitiveness of the agriculture and forestry industries (e.g. restructuring holdings, improving human capital and product quality).

Axis 2 of the Fund—on which a minimum of 25 per cent of allocated funds must be spent—aims to support land management measures designed to enhance the environment and the countryside (e.g. agri-environment schemes, animal welfare commitments).

Axis 3 of the Fund—on which a minimum of 15 per cent of allocated funds must be spent—aims to support policies that target improvements in the quality of life in rural areas (e.g. basic services provision, rural heritage conservation) and promote economic diversification towards non-agricultural activities (e.g. tourism).

A minimum of 5 per cent of EAFRD funds are ring-fenced for LEADER initiatives across the three axes. Under the LEADER approach, local action groups can secure funding for local development projects.

---

6   LEADER is the acronym for "Liaison Entre Actions pour le Développement de l'Economie Rurale", which translates as "linkage between actions for the development of the rural economy".

14. Each Member State's overall allocation[7] of rural development funding from the EAFRD is made up of a number of elements: a share of the funds replacing the guarantee element of the European Agricultural Guidance and Guarantee Fund (EAGGF), receipts from the compulsory modulation of direct payments under Pillar I, and transfers from the Structural Funds component of the EU budget.[8] The European Commission uses a historic allocation key to distribute the main element of the EAFRD budget among the EU-15. This historic allocation key is based on rural development expenditure in each Member State during the mid-1990s, and has been inherited from the EAGGF regime previously in place.

The Health Check

15. During the negotiations on the 2003 reform package, a number of review clauses were built into the final agreement as a condition for securing consensus. These review clauses are the basis for the Commission's "Health Check", which is intended to explore what further policy adjustments may be required as a result of market developments, a shifting international context, and the enlargement of the European Union.

16. The Health Check was formally launched by the European Commission on 20 November 2007, when it issued a Communication outlining its approach to the review.[9] In an accompanying speech, the European Commissioner for Agriculture, Mariann Fischer Boel, made clear that the Commission "does not see the CAP Health Check as a 'new reform'."[10] But she also stressed that "the Health Check is more than 'fine-tuning'". The Commissioner argued that the Health Check should be viewed as "a policy initiative in its own right, which will cover necessary adjustments and simplifications for the period 2009 to 2013." She added that the initiative should also be seen as "a stepping-stone towards the Mid-Term Review of the European Union's Financial Perspectives—which will examine priorities for after 2013."

17. The forthcoming EU budget review (on which more below) is expected to precipitate a debate about EU spending, the largest single share of which has traditionally been allocated to the CAP. This process should prompt closer scrutiny of the purpose of the CAP, and its effectiveness in achieving the goals set out for it. In this report, we therefore examine the Commission's Health Check proposals in this wider context.

Funding the CAP

18. The expenditure side of the EC[11] budget is organised around a multi-annual Financial Perspective, which sets out expenditure limits both in total and for broad headings, over time. Each Financial Perspective is formally agreed through an Inter-Institutional Agreement (IIA)—an agreement between the Commission, the Council and the European Parliament. The current Financial Perspective runs from 2007 to 2013, and is based on the Inter-Institutional Agreement reached in 2006.

---

[7] For a detailed breakdown by Member State of Community support for rural development over the 2007–2013 Financial Perspective, see Commission Decision 2006/636/EC of 12 September 2006.

[8] Commission Decision 2006/636/EC sets out the allocations by member state for the period 2007–2013.

[9] 'Preparing for the "Health Check" of the CAP Reform', COM (2007) 722.

[10] "The Health Check of the Common Agricultural Policy: fit for new opportunities", Speech by Mariann Fischer Boel before the Agriculture Committee of the European Parliament, 20 November 2007, SPEECH 07/727

[11] Technically, the budget remains the EC, not EU, budget. If ratified, the Lisbon Treaty would change this.

19.   Each Financial Perspective breaks expenditure down into several broad categories (budget headings). Budget heading 2 allocates funding to the 'Preservation and Management of Natural Resources'. It is the largest single item of expenditure, and the main budget line for funding the Common Agricultural Policy.

The Brussels Ceiling

20.   In 2002, France's then President, Jacques Chirac, and Germany's then Chancellor, Gerhard Schröder, agreed that spending on Pillar I of the CAP should not rise by more than 1 per cent a year in cash terms until the end of the next Financial Perspective in 2013. This agreement is known as the Brussels Ceiling and was endorsed by the European Council in October 2002. In practice, it means that Pillar I expenditure is treated as frozen until 2013.

Enlargement and the Financial Discipline Mechanism

21.   When the 2003 CAP reforms were negotiated, it was anticipated that the combined effect of the Brussels ceiling and the admission of up to 12 new members to the EU would put substantial pressure on the CAP budget. The reforms therefore made provision for a "financial discipline mechanism", which reduces Single Farm Payments by the percentage necessary to keep total Pillar I expenditure below the agreed Brussels ceiling. Until 2013, the mechanism would apply only to payments to farmers in the EU-15. It would not operate in the new Member States until they became entitled to receive full direct payments in 2013. Box 4 explains how Single Farm Payments are being phased in in the new Member States.

22.   Due to unexpected savings on market management (particularly intervention costs) as a result of the boom in some agricultural commodity markets, it has thus far not proved necessary to apply the financial discipline mechanism. Forecasts now suggest that it is unlikely to come into effect before 2010.

BOX 4

Single Farm Payments in the new Member States

In the Member States that joined the EU since 2004, the funds available for direct payments under Pillar I of the CAP are being phased in over a period of nine years. They are allocated a percentage of the funds they would be entitled to were the transitional arrangements not to apply. This percentage rises from 25 per cent in 2004 to 100 per cent by 2013.

All the new Member States were given the option of allocating direct payments using a **Single Area Payment Scheme** (**SAPS**) rather than the Single Payment Scheme (SPS) used by the EU-15. Under the SAPS, subsidies are allocated on the basis of uniform payments per hectare of agricultural land. All the new Member States except Malta and Slovenia use the SAPS, but are currently required to make the transition to the SPS by 2010 (for 2004 entrants) or 2011 (for 2007 entrants). This provision may be reviewed.

The 2005 Budget Deal

23.   The resources (income) side of the EC budget is agreed through an Own Resources Decision (ORD)—a unanimous Council decision following consultation with the European Parliament. Negotiations on revenue and expenditure, and thus the overall size and composition of the EC budget culminate in a political agreement at the European Council. The political agreement on the 2007–2013 Financial Perspective and on a new ORD was reached at the European Council meeting in Brussels in December 2005.

24. As part of progressive reductions in the overall level of EU expenditure during the course of the negotiations, the level of spending on the CAP was cut. Most of the cuts came from expenditure allocated to rural development under Pillar II, rather than from the expenditure allocated to Pillar I. The final allocation for rural development under Pillar II over the 2007–2013 period was €69.75 billion, down from the €74 billion proposed by the Luxembourg Presidency in June 2005, which was in turn lower than the original Commission proposal of €88.7 billion. By way of comparison, the budget for Pillar I was cut from €301.174 billion (the original Commission proposal) to €293.105 billion (the final Council compromise).

The Budget Review

25. The December 2005 agreement on the EC budget stipulated that the Commission should be asked to carry out a full review of EU spending and resources, reporting in 2008/9. The exact wording of the mandate invites the Commission 'to undertake a full, wide ranging review covering all aspects of EU spending, including the CAP, and of resources, including the UK rebate, to report in 2008/9. On the basis of such a review, the European Council can take decisions on all the subjects covered by the review.'[12]

26. The Commission has recently issued a consultation paper as part of its preparatory work on the budget review.[13] Our report is intended to contribute to the debate on future priorities for EU spending that is expected to ensue.

Other Influences on the CAP: WTO Negotiations

27. The widespread decoupling of farm payments as part of the 2003 CAP reforms means that most direct subsidies to farmers now qualify for "green box" status in world trade negotiations under the WTO. Green box subsidies must either not distort trade, or distort it only minimally. Box 5 explains how the WTO boxes work.

28. However, the coupled payments that remain, together with the market intervention and price support instruments that are still in use, continue to distort production and trade. Export subsidies encourage the release of surpluses onto world markets, thus pushing world prices downwards, which affects third-country producers. Meanwhile import tariffs protect the EU's internal market in agricultural commodities, affecting third-country producers who wish to export into the EU market, and keeping prices within the EU artificially high, which affects EU consumers.

29. If successful, the current Doha round of world trade negotiations would target some of these forms of support. Early on in the negotiations, the EU made a commitment to phase out all its export subsidies by 2013, and to begin removing some of those subsidies two or three years earlier. The European Commissioner for Trade, Peter Mandelson, told us that there is also room for agreement on the "green box" that would allow the EU to continue with the Single Farm Payment scheme and its rural development programme. On market access, he suggested that the proposed ranges of the tiered formula[14] for tariff reductions "are a perfectly acceptable basis for political agreement" (Q 747).

---

[12] Council of the European Union, Financial Perspective 2007–13, 19 December 2005, 15915/05, Pa. 80.

[13] 'Reforming the Budget, Changing Europe—A Public Consultation Paper in View of the 2008/2009 Budget Review', Communication from the Commission, 12 September 2007, SEC (2007) 1188.

[14] Reducing tariffs through a tiered formula means setting a number of tariff bands to which different rates of reduction apply.

30. However, the treatment of sensitive products[15] remains "the most sensitive area for our Member States and the most difficult for us to handle internally within the EU". Negotiations on geographical indications[16] are also proving tense—Mr Mandelson admits that the EU does "not have many friends" on geographical indications, which are "very, very important for our southern Member States" (Q 747).

31. The Commissioner stressed, however, that "there is nothing happening in the Health Check that I would either want or expect to impinge on the offers we are making in this trade round"(Q 753). He insisted that the EU was "at the outer limit of what we can offer in those trade talks and I would not ask for or expect any Health Check to deliver a better offer" (Q 754).

BOX 5
What are the WTO Trade Boxes?

In the context of WTO negotiations, subsidies are categorized into coloured "boxes" that indicate the degree to which they are considered acceptable. Exceptions apply for developing countries.

Amber Box

Domestic support measures considered to distort production and trade (with some exceptions) fall into this category. Examples are measures that support prices or subsidies that are directly linked to production quantities.

These types of subsidies are subject to limits. Those WTO members that exceed the limit are committed to reductions.

Blue Box

Agricultural subsidies that would qualify for the Amber Box, but are linked to conditions designed to limit production, fall into the more acceptable Blue Box instead.

At present there are no limits on spending on blue box subsidies, but this is under negotiation in the current round of trade talks.

Green Box

In order to qualify for the Green Box, subsidies must not distort trade, or at most cause limited distortion. They must be government-funded (rather than the result of higher prices charged to consumers), and must not involve price support. Subsidies that fall into this category tend not to target particular products. They include direct income supports for farmers that are not linked to (i.e. are decoupled from) current production levels or prices. They also include environmental protection and regional development subsidies.

There are currently no limits on spending on Green Box subsidies. There is disagreement among WTO members, however, over the types of payments that should qualify for the Green Box. Some countries argue that the current criteria are too lax, and that certain types of subsidies (e.g. direct payments to producers, income safety-nets, subsidised income insurance) should not qualify as they do distort trade more than minimally. Others view the current criteria as adequate and indeed wish to expand their scope, for example to include payments for environmental protection and animal welfare commitments.

---

[15] Products nominated by WTO members as exempt from tariff reduction formulas by mutual agreement. There are two elements to such exemptions: the number of tariff lines that may be included under the sensitive product clause, and the percentage deviation from the agreed general tariff for the commodity sector that is permitted.

[16] An indication that identifies a product as originating in the territory of a WTO Member, or a region or locality in that territory, and where a given quality, reputation or other characteristic of the product is essentially attributable to its geographical origin, for example Scotch whisky or Parma ham.

CHAPTER 2: THE PURPOSE OF THE CAP POST-2013

32. As part of our inquiry, we invited witnesses to set out what the long-term objectives of the Common Agricultural Policy should be. In this chapter, we review some of the responses received, and present the conclusions we have drawn from them. With this long-term vision in mind, we move on—in the next two chapters—to an examination of how the instruments through which the CAP is delivered may need to be adapted.

33. Broadly speaking, the evidence we received drew attention to three types of goal for the CAP: economic goals, environmental goals, and social goals. Each is addressed in a separate section below.

Economic Goals

34. The most elementary function of the CAP is its role in maintaining a Single Market in agricultural commodities within the EU, for example by setting ground rules for competition and state aid. DEFRA insisted that the CAP should secure "a free, fair and level playing field throughout the EU for farmers to produce and market their goods in a single market, as in other sectors of the economy", and added that "the integration of agriculture within EU competition policy on the same basis as for other sectors with rules set at the EU level" would be central to this (Written Evidence, Para 2).

35. Among most of our witnesses, there was strong support for the Common Agricultural Policy's role in creating a level playing field across the EU for producers of agricultural commodities. Kirsten Holm Svendsen of the Danish Permanent Representation to the EU explained that from the point of view of the Danish government, "if you do want to have a Common Agricultural Policy it has to go on being common because re-nationalisation of support is not something that would be helpful to us at all. We all know the theories about state aid and competing via your Treasury, but it is not a situation where we would be a winner, because we are just a small country with a very small economy" (Q 456). This was a sentiment shared by producer groups in the UK, who remain broadly sceptical of moves towards re-nationalising aspects of the CAP, because they believe the UK Government would be less generous towards the domestic industry than the governments of other Member States (Q 688).

36. UK producer groups expressed concern at what they view as an erosion of the "commonality" of the CAP, notably as a result of the application of voluntary modulation. NFU President Peter Kendall emphasized that "we have ended up with a CAP which, to me, is less 'common'. Certainly in my farming memory—for the 24 years I have been farming—we do have, even within the island of the United Kingdom, four different systems. We also have a very varied system in Europe" (Q 104). Voluntary modulation was the most commonly cited example of diminishing commonality. Andy Robertson of the NFU Scotland told us that "there are only two Member States in the whole of the 27 which are applying voluntary modulation, the UK and Portugal, which means that in practice UK farmers and Portuguese farmers are having their direct support reduced to a level which is significantly below that for farmers in the rest of the EU, and given that one of the whole points of having a single market is that people are trading on level terms, that immediately seems to us to undermine the principle of a free market" (Q 357). Further downstream in the food chain, the Food and Drink

Federation also emphasised "how important it is that we have a level playing field within the EU in order for our industry to remain competitive in the UK" (Q 812).

37. **W₂ share our witnesses' view that the "commonality" of the CAP should be its central feature. The regulation of the Single Market in agricultural commodities within the EU should therefore continue to be the primary role of a Common Agricultural Policy. However, we also note that there is a difficult balancing act to be struck between preserving the "commonality" of the CAP and responding to calls for greater flexibility in the way common goals are delivered in different Member States and indeed in different regions within each Member State.**

38. A much more controversial issue is whether the Common Agricultural Policy should aim to foster an agricultural sector that is capable of competing on world markets without subsidy and without a greater level of protection (through import tariffs) than that accorded to other economic sectors. For those who do not endorse this objective, the question becomes: to what extent, and on what grounds, should agriculture continue to be treated as exceptional?

39. Our witnesses took a wide range of views on these issues. The main exponent of the view that the agriculture should not be treated any differently than are other sectors of the economy was the UK government. DEFRA proposed that "within 10 to 15 years, European agriculture should be internationally competitive without reliance on subsidy or protection" (Written Evidence, Para. 1). Murray Sherwin, Director-General of the New Zealand Ministry for Agriculture and Forestry, pointed out to us that "we are all members of agencies like the WTO, IMF and OECD, whose starting principles are around the benefits of trade liberalization and free trade" and yet one might wonder "how come these organisations have so many members, because they patently do not seem to believe the principles that they have signed up for" (Q 307). He went on to assure us that "there really are gains to be had for welfare" from agricultural trade liberalization, albeit alongside "some awkward distributional issues."

40. Three main arguments were put to us for why agriculture should not be exposed to international competition in the same way that other sectors have been. The most frequent contention was that producers of agricultural commodities in the EU are forced to comply with a series of environmental, health and animal welfare standards that place them at a competitive disadvantage vis-à-vis third-country producers who are not required to meet similarly exacting standards. Subsidies then serve to level the playing field, "compensating" farmers for the regulatory burden placed on them. This is a view that received some sympathy from Mariann Fischer Boel, the European Commissioner for Agriculture (Q 690), as well as receiving strong endorsement from many of the farmers' unions.[17] Dai Davies, President of NFU Cymru, argued that "if you deny us the support then certainly hand in hand with that the constraints have to disappear as well" (Q 341).

41. Peter Mandelson, the European Commissioner for Trade, did not accept this argument. He countered that "the obligations that we are placing on them

---

[17] See also Q 209.

[the European farming industry], the standards that we require of them, are designed to make them competitive" and are "going where the market is heading in any case". He explained that "we are competing in a very, very tough global economy with premium products, added value, high standards", noting that "in that sense, agriculture is no different from any other production sector in Europe" (Q 756).

42.   Underpinning these positions we detected contrasting views on the extent to which market forces should be allowed to shape the long-term structure of the industry. Commissioner Fischer Boel stressed that she did not want to see an industrialised agricultural sector in Europe, but instead wanted to promote "a diversified sector, where there is room for the small ones, for those who want to specialise in fruit and vegetables, organic or whatever, and the big competitive ones as well" (Q 690). She was consequently concerned that "if you take away all the direct payments we have no way of securing that we can maintain diversification".

43.   Commissioner Mandelson appeared to be less wary of structural change, noting that "our agricultural sector in Europe is both shrinking and becoming more efficient and competitive as it becomes more market-oriented" (Q 754). He predicted that "we will be importing more of what we cannot compete with on efficiency and cost and price terms through domestic production" but emphasized that "that does not mean to say that the agricultural sector in Europe is disappearing." Instead, it will mean producing "those things that we are best at and good at exporting", resulting in the end in "a more market-oriented, more competitive, and therefore more sustainable agricultural sector" (Q 754).

44.   Other witnesses argued that the agriculture sector would have to continue to receive special treatment if "food security" was to be achieved (Q 807). The combined effect of having less land available for food production as a result of climate change and land being used to grow energy crops, and growing demand for agricultural commodities from emerging economies like China and India, could lead to pressures on food supplies. John Don, former Chairman of the Scottish Rural Property and Business Association, suggested that due to pressures from the third world on food supplies "it is going to become increasingly important that we have a strategic supply of food and fuel in European production". The policy implication was that "we should support in a long-term way the continuation of primary production throughout Europe" (Q 212).

45.   Professor Alan Buckwell of the Country Land and Business Association also made a case for putting food security at the core of the EU's agricultural and environmental policy, but explained that "by European food security what we mean is protecting the long run food production capacity of the European Union" (Q 208). He emphasised that "we are not talking about European self-sufficiency; we are talking about the capacity to produce." Others, however, did have self-sufficiency in mind. Yves Madre of the French Permanent Representation to the European Union told us that in future, the CAP should secure "food independence" for Europe (Q 499). The French government is of the view that "food is a political tool and if you have a shortage of food you will be weak" (Q 501). It consequently insists that "we must avoid being dependent on other countries for all that we need, only for

the very minimum necessary, and producing in our own European territories" (Q 504).[18]

46. The UK Government does not share these witnesses' interpretations of what food security might entail. Sonia Phippard of DEFRA emphasised that "it is quite important that food security is not confused with either self-sufficiency or national security. The UK, and indeed the EU, have relied very heavily on effective trading relationships as part of our food security for many years." Her colleague Simon Harding explained that "there are a huge variety of threats to our food security and food supplies and only some of those threats are of a nature that would make it helpful to actually grow lots of food on your own sovereign territories." He added that "there is not really a very direct connection between how much food you grow domestically and the level of security that you attach to your suppliers of food. There are a great many other influences such as energy supplies, logistical systems, the possibility of terrorist attacks, etc." (Q 13).

47. Mr Harding also assured us that most studies of the probable impact of radical trade liberalisation on agricultural production in Europe "seem to indicate that changes in the output of European agriculture could be less than ten per cent and could be between ten and 20 per cent and is less likely to be any more than that". He explained that "if you apply those levels of changes to what we already produce, you do not get an alarming picture of moving into a marginal food supply." DEFRA has published figures suggesting that the UK is about 60 per cent self-sufficient in food, and about 70 per cent self-sufficient in indigenous products.[19] Mr Harding pointed out that "if you were to look at our nutritional requirements and ask the question: 'Are we going to starve or feel hungry?', the answer to that would be a great deal different and the relevant figure would be a great deal higher"(Q 13).

48. **We believe that the drive towards a more market-oriented agriculture should continue. In the long term, the CAP should aim to foster a farming sector that is capable of standing on its own feet, competing in open international markets without subsidy or special protection. We acknowledge the likelihood of greater demand for agricultural commodities in future, and believe that this presents an opportunity for the European farming industry. The distorting effect of subsidies will in our view hinder the EU agriculture sector's ability to respond to, and profit from, the expected increase in global demand for agricultural products. The CAP should instead aim to steer the industry towards a position from which it can take full advantage of a future boom in commodities prices. In our view, this means moving away from the distortions that a managed and protected internal market for agricultural commodities creates and sustains.**

---

[18] Some Council delegations have also stressed the "strategic role of agriculture for the security of supply of 500 million Europeans" (Press Release 15333/07 on the Agriculture and Fisheries Council Meeting held in Brussels on 26–27 November 2007, p. 9). See too the Spanish position set out in Q 551, and the Polish position set out in Q 807.

[19] Self-sufficiency calculations are based on UK agriculture's ability to meet domestic consumer demand rather than the calorie requirements of domestic consumers. In light of over-consumption, food wastage and the possibility of switching to more calorie-efficient foods, the UK's level of self-sufficiency may be higher than these figures suggest—as the witness goes on to point out. See "Food Security and the UK: An Evidence and Analysis Paper" published by DEFRA in December 2006, pp. 33–34.

49. **We were not persuaded by the argument that the risk of future food shortages should be hedged against by freezing current production patterns. In our judgement, food scarcity is likely to be a function of income rather than of production capacity. If the supply shortages anticipated by some witnesses do materialise, those most at risk are consumers on low incomes in the developing world.**[20]

Social Goals

50. The third reason witnesses gave for why agriculture should be treated differently than other sectors of the economy was that it generates social and environmental benefits (positive externalities) that are not rewarded by the market, resulting in what economists call "market failure". In this section and the next, we review the arguments put to us in these respects, and examine whether the CAP should aim to secure social and environmental, as well as economic goals.

51. A number of witnesses referred to the CAP's role in supporting rural communities, particularly in remote areas. Andy Robertson, Chief Executive of NFU Scotland, pointed out that "an awful lot of what agriculture does is not just about food production but it is about its effect on the rural economy and on rural communities" (Q 339). This view received endorsement from Richard Lochhead, Scotland's Cabinet Secretary for Rural Affairs, who explained that support for Less Favoured Areas[21] delivers social benefits and wider public benefits (Appendix 4, Para. 9). Yves Madre of the French Permanent Representation to the EU concurred, noting that "agriculture is not only agricultural goods, it is a matter of the environment, landscapes, society" and that as a result "we will never succeed in applying exactly the same rules" as in other sectors (Q 536).

52. Some witnesses were of the view that the support payments channelled to farmers through the CAP played a vital role in preventing rural depopulation. The French government believes that the CAP should "ensure that the balance between territories within the European Union will not be destroyed and in all regions we will keep enough people, enough agricultural activities," Mr Madre told us (Q 504). On a similar note, Mr Valentin Almansa de Lara of the Spanish Permanent Representation to the EU explained that Spain "wants to see people living in the countryside" and believes "agriculture must be the engine" (QQ 554, 555). "Our aim is that people in rural areas have money, have benefits, and can live there with their activities", he added. Closer to home, his sentiment was echoed by Andrew Douglas of the Scottish Rural Property and Business Association, who noted that "in Scotland we are an 85 per cent ess favoured area, and we have had the less favoured area payment for many years. We have always argued that that payment is a payment to keep people in the glens and valleys" (Q 211).

53. Mr Almansa de Lara was sceptical of whether the market alone could deliver these outcomes: "If we leave it to the market, who will produce 2,000 litres

---

[20] See for example the Food and Agriculture Organization (FAO) of the United Nations' "Food Outlook", November 2007 and the FAO Director-General's comments at a press conference held on 17 December 2007 at the Organization's Rome headquarters.

[21] A term used to describe an area with permanent natural handicaps (e.g. unfavourable soil or climate conditions, mountainous terrain), in danger of depopulation or subject to environmental restrictions. Since 1975 (in the case of areas subject to environmental restrictions, since 1999), these areas have been eligible for additional financial aid under the CAP.

[of milk] a year or 20,000 litres [of milk] a year in the high mountains? Nobody." Nor was he convinced of the feasibility of pursuing the desired goals without subsidising agricultural activity. He suggested that this would amount to treating farmers like "the Indians in North America who are paid to be Indians on a reserve. You need some economic activity. They need to be active in their business and their business is agriculture" (Q 557).

54. Several witnesses stressed agriculture's role in maintaining a critical mass of population and amenities in remote areas. Andy Robertson of the NFU Scotland suggested that in his experience "if there was any reduction in the number of farmers then you started to lose critical mass and you started to lose things like schools and shops and so on. Certainly in the remoter rural communities it is fair to say that agriculture is very central" to the economic and social wellbeing of these communities (Q 328). Mr Almansa de Lara made the link between a lack of infrastructure and the demographic composition of rural areas, noting that "we are seeing more and more older farmers on the farms and no young people". Young people, he suggested, were put off by the fact that "in the very remote areas of Spain you will have no cinemas, no hospital, no disco, no girls," creating "a real problem" (Q 558).

55. Subsidising farming through the CAP protects both agricultural and non-agricultural jobs in disadvantaged areas, we were told. Representing the Polish government, Mr Beniamin Gawlik explained that if Polish farmers with holdings of less than one hectare were denied support, "there will be no real alternative for those people" (Q 788). Walter Duebner of the German Permanent Representation made a similar argument with respect to agricultural activity in Germany's Eastern Länder, claiming that "it is better to keep the money on the farms because sometimes they have more employees than they would need if they had a sophisticated structure" (Q 410).

56. Other witnesses drew attention to the "multiplier effect" of farming activity. Mary James of NFU Cymru cited independent evidence on Wales suggesting that "for each farming job there are ten full-time equivalents produced in rural areas" (Q 348). Andy Robertson of NFU Scotland pointed out that in Scotland, this meant that "if you did not have an active farming industry there and if you pulled away all the subsidies and goods it seeks to produce it would not just affect farmers, it would affect an awful lot of other jobs" (Q 326).

57. From the perspective of some of our Welsh and Scottish witnesses, agriculture—and by extension, the CAP—also has a role to play in preserving traditional cultures and communities. The President of NFU Cymru, Dai Davies, drew our attention to the fact that in Wales, "the majority of people involved in agriculture still speak Welsh and it's a major issue for us in Wales if we wish to retain the language and our heritage"(Q 326). He also maintained that if subsidies were withdrawn, "we would not be able to sustain the same type of people or the same type of communities in those rural areas that we have now"(Q 329). He feared that instead, these areas might "become dormitories for people who had decided to retire and go down the route of the good life in peaceful areas or you would have commuters." Mike Rumbles, Rural Affairs Spokesperson for the Scottish Liberal Democrats, made a similar point, stressing that "especially in more

remote rural areas, for example in traditional crofting communities, we don't want traditional ways of life turned around"(Appendix 5, Para. 5).

58. **We recognize that many Member States are currently relying on CAP funds—and particularly on direct payments under Pillar I—to secure social policy goals. However, we believe that many of the problems being addressed—such as the lack of employment opportunities in remote rural areas, or the fragility of rural communities—deserve to be tackled in their own right. Direct payments to farmers and landowners are an indirect, and in our view poorly-focused, instrument with which to address these challenges. Agricultural interests should not be equated with rural interests: channelling financial support through the agriculture sector may not be the most efficient and effective way of sustaining rural communities.**

59. **The needs of rural communities are likely to be very different across different Member States and across different regions within each country. Agriculture may or may not have a role to play in meeting those needs, and different Member States will wish to give varying levels of prominence to the agriculture sector in their overall rural development strategy. For this reason too, we believe that uniform direct payments to farmers under Pillar I of the CAP are not the appropriate vehicle for the implementation of a diverse set of national rural policies.**

60. **We believe that some of these goals—such as the diversification of the rural economy—would be better pursued through Pillar II of the CAP (and indeed provision is already made for such actions under the EAFRD), while others—such as the structural problems in the rural areas of the new Member States—would be better tackled through other EU programmes (e.g. Structural and Cohesion Funds). Social and cultural objectives, however, are in our view too numerous and too diverse to be pursued exclusively through EU-level programmes. They should be addressed primarily at a national, or even sub-national level, at domestic taxpayers' expense.**

Environmental Goals

61. There was consensus among witnesses from the environmental sector that agricultural activity can produce positive environmental side-effects, and that in the absence of market compensation for these externalities, farmers should be rewarded financially for at least some of the environmental public goods that their activity generates. This is already a feature of the CAP, for example as part of cross-compliance in Pillar I, and through agri-environment schemes in Pillar II.

62. Dr Helen Phillips, CEO of Natural England, proposed that "EU policy should be directed towards securing environmental goods and services that are not rewarded by the prices paid for in our food"(Q 143). Natural England envisages "a new social contract between farmers and the rest of society: one where farmers see one of their primary roles as the protection and stewardship of the countryside, in return for which taxpayers are willing to make that investment in the longer term." Hannah Bartram of the Environment Agency took a similar view, advocating that public money should be spent on "the provision of public goods and services. We are obviously particularly interested in clean water, robust soils, functioning

flood plains, but also the wildlife/access/landscape issues. We feel that support for these goods is justified when the market does not value them, and therefore fails to deliver them at an optimal level" (Q 184).

63.   Dr Mark Avery of the Royal Society for the Protection of Birds also highlighted a perceived market failure in this area, arguing that "agriculture is different from other industries. Agriculture produces wildlife, landscape and other public goods, providing you get the right type of agriculture, and it is fair for the public to support farmers to produce that because there is no market for farmers to tap into" (Q 57). Meanwhile David Young of Natural England warned that "a consequence of not having a CAP is that we place at risk all of those public goods that will not be delivered by the market mechanisms" (Q 145).

64.   Other witnesses pointed out that the environmental externalities of farming activity contributed to the maintenance of landscapes that the tourist industry relies upon. Dai Davies, President of NFU Cymru, emphasised that "farming does not only produce food, it has a responsibility for the environment and the environment seems very important for tourism coming into parts of Wales" (Q 326). Ian Woodhurst of the Campaign to Protect Rural England pointed out that "when you look at the *Visit Britain* website there is a lot of play made about the quality of the landscapes," but "there is actually no mention at all of what any of this has to do with farming or the fact that farming systems are producing and still maintaining these environmental assets and these landscapes" (Q 254).

65.   **We recognize that certain types of farming activity can generate environmental benefits that are valued by society at large but whose value is not reflected in market prices for agricultural products. It does not automatically follow, however, that farmers should receive financial rewards for the environmental public goods that their activity helps to provide.**

66.   Rather than being prompted with financial rewards, producers in other sectors of the economy tend to be subject to regulation that penalizes them if they fail to deliver on environmental objectives. Baroness Young of Old Scone, Chief Executive of the Environment Agency, acknowledged that "you can substitute the words 'miners' or 'the British car industry' for 'farmers' and it sounds like madness". She insisted that "the reality, however, is that the difference between the farming industry and land management generally and any other economic sector is that they are *the* guardians, *the* operators, over a fundamental slice of the environment, probably impacting on all three environmental media: land, air and water" (Q 186).

67.   "Why should consumers pay for the environment where other businesses are not paid to obey environmental laws is a very good question," conceded Allan Buckwell of the Country Land and Business Association. In his view, "it is because land managers, farmers, steward the environment the way that no other business does", but also "because consumers will not pay in their food". He thus argued that "what people say they want in environmental standards they do not match in their purchases in the supermarket. If we do not provide some assistance to the deliverers of these environmental services then we will not get these services" (QQ 241–242).

68.   Some witnesses expressed scepticism over whether the desired environmental outcomes could be secured through regulation. Professor Buckwell insisted

that "in terms of achievement and results you will find that if you try to bring about the environmental standards you want by pure regulation you will not achieve it" (Q 245). Tom Oliver told us that the Campaign to Protect Rural England's "strong feeling is that it is much more effective to incentivise people than it is to regulate them into doing things" (Q 265).

69. Others, however, pointed out that distinctions could be drawn among different environmental objectives, some of which could be met by regulation alone, and some of which could not. Dr Helen Phillips of Natural England pointed out to us that Statutory Management Requirements, one of two elements of the cross compliance conditions that farmers must meet if they are to be eligible for Single Farm Payments, are "legal requirements that are effectively being paid for through the Single Farm Payment" (Q 148). She argued that "we do not want to be either subsidising or consequently inflicting undue regulation on people for meeting basic operating requirements" but should instead consider how to protect additional requirements, such as the Good Agricultural and Environmental Condition requirements that make up the second facet of cross compliance (QQ 148–149).

70. A compelling argument in favour of drawing such a distinction is that "at the end of the day, we do not by any manner of means want to be paying for every environmental good and service we want. If we get ourselves into that position—let us be frank—there will not be enough money to go round," Dr Phillips warned (Q 147).

71. **We believe that the CAP should continue to promote farming methods and practices that will result in environmental benefits. Given limited public resources, we see merit in drawing a distinction between environmental outcomes that can be secured through regulation—such as the control of emissions and pollution—and those that are unlikely to be delivered without financial incentives—such as the positive management of a wildlife habitat.**

72. Dr Phillips explained that in the United Kingdom, the funding formula for securing environmental goods and services from land managers is based on income foregone. She pointed out that this implies that when commodity prices go up, the inevitable reality is that "you can buy less" (Q 152).

73. **We recognise the inherent difficulty in determining which environmental goods and services should be paid for from the public purse, and in putting a price on their value to society.[22] We expect that these valuations may change over time, notably in the event of food price inflation. We consequently recommend that these decisions should be taken at a national level wherever possible, albeit on the basis of a menu of admissible uses for CAP funds defined at the EU level.[23]**

74. While most of our witnesses chose to dwell on agriculture's positive environmental externalities, the sector also has very considerable negative impacts. It is accountable for nine per cent of greenhouse gas emissions across the EU, and is the second-highest producer of methane in the UK

---

[22] DEFRA has commissioned studies that attempt to place an economic value on environmental goods. See for example 'Economic Valuation of Environmental Impacts in the Severely Disadvantaged Areas', a report produced by the Economics for the Environment Consultancy (EFTEC) for DEFRA, 3 January 2006.

[23] See also Para. 207 of this report.

after the energy industry (Q 164). This means that "agriculture, like all other industries, will have to be looking at its carbon emissions and looking at ways to do its job with lower emissions", Dr Avery of the RSPB told us. But he was keen to stress that this provides an opportunity as well as a challenge for the industry: "there are some quite big opportunities for land management in terms of looking at whether places like the uplands have a different future, which is in being carbon sinks, and managing upland peat and soils in different ways to stop them being degraded, to stop them drying out, to stop them emitting greenhouse gases". He concluded that "it may be that upland farmers will be paid for farming carbon rather than farming sheep in 20 years' time", and added that "flood risk management may be another thing which is produced in that way" (Q 92).

75. **Climate change considerations will clearly have to figure prominently among the future environmental objectives of the CAP. The EU's agriculture sector will need to improve its impact on the environment, but climate change also presents a business opportunity for the industry, which it must be encouraged to seize. In the long run, the best way to secure progress towards both goals may be to integrate agriculture in an EU-wide greenhouse gas emissions trading scheme. We consequently recommend that this possibility be given further consideration as a matter of urgency.**

CHAPTER 3: PILLAR I AFTER THE HEALTH CHECK

76. In its Communication on the Health Check published on 20 November 2007, the Commission set out the areas in which it would like to see further reform of the CAP.[24] Legislative proposals are expected to follow in May 2008. In the sections that follow, we examine the Commission's main proposals.

Basis for Single Farm Payments

77. One of the central features of the 2003 reform of the CAP was the pooling of subsidy entitlements previously linked to individual commodity regimes into a single payment. In implementing this so-called Single Payment Scheme, Member States could choose to allocate payments on a historic basis (linked to production during a reference period) or on a regional/area basis (linked to the number of eligible hectares farmed), or a mix of the two. In the UK, England has implemented an area-based payments system, while Scotland, Wales and Northern Ireland have opted to allocate payments on an historic basis.[25]

Commission Proposals

78. In its Communication, the Commission has indicated that it would like to see Member States adjusting their chosen model "towards a flatter rate during the period from 2009 to 2013."[26] Commissioner Fischer Boel explained that "the Single Payment Scheme has been implemented in many different ways in many different Member States and personally I think we should work towards a more flat rate system, a less complicated system, where you have a payment of the same value, or entitlements of the same value, linked to the area". The reason for making this adjustment, she suggested, was that "from a psychological point of view, I think we will face difficulties in 2013 or 2018, just to mention a year, explaining why two neighbouring farmers get different payments with the same conditions for production because the former owner had dairy production in 2002. That is going to be difficult to explain to taxpayers" (Q 685).

Witnesses' Views

79. Many of our witnesses accepted the logic of this argument. Martin Haworth told us that the NFU also envisaged that the next step would be "the whole of Europe going to some sort of area payment", and agreed that "you cannot justify a historic allocation for very long" (Q 119). Walter Duebner of the German Permanent Representation to the EU told us that Germany, which currently operates a hybrid system, intends to move to an area-based payment during the period 2010–2013 (Q 404). Beniamin Gawlik told us

---

[24] COM (2007) 722.

[25] England technically operates a dynamic hybrid system, meaning that it will gradually move to flat-rate payments. Denmark, Germany and Finland also operate dynamic hybrid systems. Luxembourg and Sweden operate static hybrid systems, meaning that they intend to maintain mixed systems. Of the other Member States who use the Single Payment Scheme, nine use historical models, and two (Slovenia and Malta) use area-based models. The remaining new Member States use the Single Area Payment Scheme (SAPS) rather than the SPS.

[26] COM (2007) 722, Para. 2.1.

that the Polish government sees the possibility of moving towards flat-rate payments across the EU as a "positive signal", since it indicates a recognition on the part of the Commission that the simplified flat-rate system employed by Poland and other Member States that joined the EU in 2004 and 2007 is quite efficient (Q 781). The system known as the Single Area Payments Scheme (SAPS) is "appreciated by farmers" and "quite easy to manage for the administration", Mr Gawlik added.

80.   Other witnesses were more cautious. In Spain, the 2003 reforms were only implemented in 2006. The Spanish government consequently feels it needs more time and more debate before any moves towards a "more or less compulsory" regional system (Q 538). Andy Robertson of the NFU Scotland accepted that "the further we get away from 2000–2004 [the reference period for the historical payments system] the more difficult it is to justify saying somebody is getting a payment because of what they did ten years ago." But he insisted that "a single area payment which simply said we are going to pay X amount per hectare regardless of where the farm is, what type of farm it is and what it would be producing" would not be valid either (Q 336). His views were echoed by the NFU Cymru and the Farmers' Union of Wales (Q 336). Richard Lochhead, Scottish Cabinet Secretary for Rural Affairs, noted that the Commission's proposal causes anxiety in Scotland, but recognized the logic of the argument and that it would therefore perhaps not be sensible to keep allocating payments on an historic basis (Appendix 4, Para. 2). He stressed however, that the transition would be important, and would take time, not least because Scotland's geography and topography are sufficiently diverse as to render a flat-rate payment unpopular and difficult to justify.

Conclusions

81.   **The logic of the Commission's argument for moving away from historic payment models is compelling, and we therefore support its proposal to encourage Member States to move towards a "flatter" and, in our view, more rational and transparent payments system. We note that the language used by the Commission is permissive, and that it intends to allow Member States to decide "whether to move to flatter rates, at which scale (Member State-wide, regional ...) and to which extent."[27] We believe that this very substantial degree of flexibility should go some way towards meeting the concerns raised.**

82.   **In the longer term, however, we are not convinced of the justification for maintaining direct payments under Pillar I, as the market and environmental objectives that we regard as the appropriate long-term aims of the CAP can in our view be pursued adequately with the instruments available under Pillar II. We therefore recommend that a progressive flattening of payments systems in the aftermath of the Health Check should in due course be accompanied by a phased reduction in direct payments over the course of the next financial perspective.**

---

[27] Commission Memo 07/476, 20 November 2007.

Upper and Lower Limits for Direct Payments

83. In the EU-27, around 80 per cent of direct payments under Pillar I of the CAP are awarded to just 20 per cent of beneficiaries.[28] This is because direct payments are linked to past production and/or the area farmed, meaning that the most productive businesses—often large in scale—receive the highest subsidies. The distribution of Single Farm Payments consequently continues to evoke controversy.

Commission Proposals

84. In its Health Check Communication, the Commission argues that the distribution of payments has become more visible since the introduction of Single Farm Payments and a recent transparency initiative whereby the names of beneficiaries and the sums awarded to them are published.[29] This has led to calls for the level of support received by a small number of large farmers to be capped. At the same time, it became clear during the implementation of the Single Payment Scheme that there are a large number of beneficiaries who receive payments that are so small that they are outweighed by the costs of administration, and that some recipients of small awards are not farmers at all.

85. The Commission therefore proposes to look into the possibility of progressively reducing subsidies above certain thresholds, while maintaining some level of subsidy even where awards are very large. With respect to the smallest payments, it proposes to consider whether a minimum level of annual payments can be introduced and/or whether the minimum area requirement can be set at a higher level. These minimum limits should be determined at Member State level, the Commission suggests, with any resulting savings being retained by the national authorities and potentially diverted to uses sanctioned by Article 69 of the 2003 CAP regulation.

Witnesses' Views

86. The UK and Germany have the greatest number of large beneficiaries from the CAP. Their governments object to the Commission's proposal to cap subsidies at the top end. Walter Duebner of the German Permanent Representation to the EU told us that "the rates of reduction discussed would cost the larger holdings in Eastern Germany approximately €300 million in income", meaning that "they would have to bear almost half of the cuts in the whole of the EU" (Q 408). The German government therefore considers the idea of capping payments based on farm size to be "unacceptable". Meanwhile the UK Government is "very opposed to upper limits", arguing that it will only lead to people spending "money on lawyers, dividing up their businesses" (Lord Rooker, Q 919). The Food and Drink Federation drew attention to the tension between capping and market-orientation (Q 817).

87. Commissioner Fischer Boel defended the proposal by insisting that "it is not a capping", but instead a "progressive reduction", meaning that "even if you are very big you will only be reduced by 45 per cent, so you will continue to get payments until the very end" (Q 701). She went on to argue that the

---

[28] Commission Memo 07/476, p.4.

[29] Commission Communication (2007) 722, p.5.

partial loss of subsidies would be offset by the economies of scale that larger farms can take advantage of, so that incentives need not be distorted.[30]

88. There was more support among our witnesses for the proposal to introduce minimum thresholds for Single Farm Payments. Poland, which like many of the new Member States has a large number of small holdings, was satisfied that the flexibility given to Member States to define what they would consider to be a farm meant that it would have "no problem" with a lower limit (Q 787). Commissioner Fischer Boel warned, however, that the proposal was "controversial in some new Member States, Romania among others, where they have not yet been through the changes in their agriculture sector" (Q 702).

Conclusions

89. **While we understand the Commission's desire to bring about a fairer distribution of subsidies by tapering off subsidies at the top end, this approach rests on an implicit assumption about what the purpose of the CAP should be that we do not share. If the Common Agricultural Policy is to target social goals—and among them, a fair income for farmers—it might indeed make sense to set up a fair, and possibly even means-tested, system of allocating subsidies. But if as we have argued, the CAP should aim to promote a competitive, market-oriented agriculture industry, then it does not make sense to introduce a measure that will penalize those who undertake the restructuring that efficiency may require. We therefore do not support the introduction of thresholds above which subsidies are progressively reduced.**

90. **By contrast, we do support the introduction of minimum thresholds for payments, as we are persuaded by the Commission's argument that it makes no sense to create subsidy entitlements that cost more to administer than the amounts being awarded. If Member States are given the flexibility to set their own minimum thresholds in the context of the structure of their farming industry, the new Member States will not be penalized.**

Cross Compliance

91. Farmers' eligibility for Single Farm Payments and other types of support is linked to their compliance with Statutory Management Requirements (SMR) and whether they meet the obligation to keep their land in Good Agricultural and Environmental Condition (GAEC)—the two facets of cross-compliance. Statutory Management requirements derive from 19 existing EU directives and regulations which all farmers have to comply with irrespective of whether they claim Single Farm Payments.

Commission Proposals

92. In its Health Check Communication, the Commission announced its intention to review the scope of cross compliance. [31] It proposes to qualify

---

[30] Note, however, that a reduction in subsidies above a certain threshold would mean that those expanding their businesses above that threshold would not reap the full return from economies of scale, as some of those returns would instead offset the reduction in subsidies. Incentives would therefore be distorted to that extent.

the Statutory Management Requirements by excluding provisions which are not directly relevant to the stated objectives of cross-compliance. It also plans to examine, and where appropriate amend, the current list of SMR and GAEC. The Commission explicitly acknowledges the need to strike the right balance between the costs and benefits of particular requirements.

Witnesses' Views

93. Most of our witnesses accepted that the introduction of cross compliance had helped to raise awareness of environmental issues on farms.[32] The Environment Agency welcomed the fact that cross compliance "sets that environmental baseline that we have been calling for for such a long time" (Q 177).[33] DEFRA referred to evidence demonstrating that cross compliance has delivered environmental benefits (Memorandum, Para. 28).

94. Producer groups felt that these improvements had been achieved at the expense of a considerable administrative burden. The Scottish NFU expressed concern that cross compliance had added to the regulatory burden faced by farming businesses without delivering proportionate benefits (Memorandum, Para. 10). COPA-COGECA's Secretary-General, Pekka Pesonen, told us that farmers did not think that the cross-compliance rules themselves were too tough, but did perceive the associated administration to be "overwhelming" (Q 575). He suggested that "there are a lot of things that we could simplify in administration in order to motivate the farmers to fulfil the legal requirements." Mr Pesonen also warned that adding new items to the cross compliance conditions could at some point tip the scales, prompting farmers to decide that "this does not add up, I will just get out of the business", at which point society would "lose the aspects that they are looking for" altogether (Q 574).

95. Also of concern to producer groups were the penalties associated with breach of the cross compliance conditions, which they regard as disproportionate. The Farmers' Union of Wales argued that "many cross compliance rules are subjective, and open to a wide range of interpretations, therefore causing disproportionate penalties to be imposed for practices that are not clearly recognisable as breaches" (Memorandum, Para.8). Some farmers, it claimed, had "lost 60 to 100 per cent of their Single Payments due to simple misunderstandings of what are subjective rules" (Memorandum, Para. 2).

96. The Environment Agency, which is the competent control authority for cross compliance in the UK, recognized that there was room for improvement in administrative arrangements (Aileen Kirmond, Q 180). With respect to penalties, Ms Kirmond proposed that "we need to retain proportionate penalties where there is serious damage but, where there is a minor breach of something, look at how we could scale that back."

97. Commissioner Fischer Boel pointed out that "Member States need to help to simplify things" too, as "there are some Member States that are over-implementing, which means adding national things on top of what was the intention" (QQ 725, 726). The evidence we received suggests that the UK is

---

[31] COM (2007) 722, Para. 2.2.

[32] Duncan Sinclair, Waitrose, Q 870; National Farmers' Union Memorandum Para. 33; Farmers' Union of Wales Memorandum Para.22; Hannah Bartram, Environment Agency, Q 173.

[33] Q 177.

among the culprits in this regard. Hannah Bartram of the Environment Agency explained that "when you look at SMRs, the standards tend to reflect the status of implementation of the relevant directive in each Member State" (Q 177). When it comes to GAEC, by contrast, "the details are much more at the Member States' discretion. Some have implemented a relatively large number of standards, and standards that go beyond what is in GAEC." This means that the level of environmental protection afforded by cross compliance varies according to the number and scope of standards adopted by each Member State, leading to "inconsistency", Ms Bartram noted. She also acknowledged that England is considered to be one of the most demanding regions of the EU when it comes to cross compliance (Q 179). With this in mind, Duncan Sinclair of Waitrose warned that "we have got to make sure that from a competitive point of view we do not saddle our industry with an extra burden of cost relative to our European counterparts" (Q 870).

98. A number of our witnesses called into question whether the SMR element of cross compliance really adds value. The Farmers' Union of Wales argued that "much of the environmental protection that is afforded by cross compliance is provided by the Statutory Management Requirements that predate Cross Compliance but have nevertheless been incorporated into Cross Compliance rules. Thus, a significant portion of cross compliance has simply sustained existing levels of environmental protection" (Memorandum, Para. 8). The Scottish NFU also took the view that "cross compliance duplicates some regulatory requirements and in fact adds to the burden of regulation, while at the same time introducing an element of double jeopardy" (Memorandum, Para. 16).

99. Natural England came to a similar conclusion, albeit for different reasons. Referring to Single Farm Payments, Helen Phillips questioned why "we allow some of that incentive money, which really needs to be earmarked very carefully for buying those things that nothing else can buy, to support and subsidise regulation" (Q 157). She went on to argue that CAP funds should not be used to reward farmers for meeting basic regulatory requirements, not least because this meant inflicting additional, undue regulation on them (Q 149). Tom Oliver also told us that while the Campaign to Protect Rural England approves of cross-compliance, it takes the view that "it is very difficult to justify paying very large sums of money per hectare to farmers to do what amount to quite meagre environmental actions" (Q 263). The Environment Agency, however, was more cautious on this front, warning that "we do not want to throw the baby out with the bathwater" (Q 177). Indeed we were told that the Agency was considering whether another SMR could be introduced under cross compliance in order to embed some aspects of the Water Framework Directive in farming practices, and that there was potentially room to expand the scope of SMRs with respect to soil management (Q 180).

100. The Farmers' Union of Wales considered that some aspects of the cross compliance regime "provide negligible or no environmental protection, and serve only to restrict farming practices unnecessarily" (Memorandum, Para. 8). It suggested that this was "particularly the case on extensive farming systems, where rules that are clearly based upon perceived problems that occur on intensive arable farms can result in significant and disproportionate penalties, despite there being no valid scientific reason for such rules to be applied."

Conclusions

101. **We welcome the Commission's intention to review the scope of cross-compliance by examining and amending the list of SMR and GAEC requirements. The evidence we have received suggests that while cross compliance has helped to deliver environmental benefits, and has been valuable in raising awareness of environmental issues among land managers, the administrative obligations associated with the regime are in some instances out of proportion to the benefits delivered. We therefore recommend that the Commission should focus on withdrawing elements from the current list of cross compliance conditions, rather than adding to it.**

102. **This is not a task for the Commission alone: Member States too need to consider whether they are trying to pack too much into cross compliance, as this is not only likely to reduce the effectiveness of the tool and sap morale among land managers, but may also lead to competitive distortions. However, we recognise that while Pillar I continues to absorb such a significant proportion of CAP spending, the environmental benefits delivered by cross compliance are an important part of the justification for public expenditure on direct payments.**

103. **In the medium term, we believe that it would be appropriate to consider whether the SMR element of cross compliance needs to be included at all. We were persuaded in this respect by Natural England's contention that financial incentives should be guarded closely, and offered only in return for environmental practices that go over and beyond what is required by law—a criterion that Statutory Management Requirements fall foul of. The lever that cross compliance offers might therefore be used more sparingly, but to better effect.**

Decoupling

104. Under the 2003 reform of the CAP, subsidies were allowed to remain partially coupled to production where it was deemed important to retain a critical mass of product supply for processing industries, or where it was judged that there was a risk of production abandonment in the absence of coupled support.

Commission Proposals

105. The Commission has made clear that it views partially coupled support as "less and less relevant", particularly in the arable crop sector, and that it therefore wishes to encourage further moves towards full decoupling, which it argues will leave producers "at least as well off as before, and most likely better off."[34] It nevertheless recognizes that partially coupled support "may retain some relevance, at least for the time being" in regions where overall levels of production are small, but important economically or environmentally. It therefore proposes that a case-by-case analysis should be undertaken at the regional level to identify whether, to what extent, and for how long support should remain partially coupled.

---

34 COM (2007) 722, Para. 2.3 and MEMO/07/476, p.3.

Witnesses' Views

106. The NFU is strongly in favour of further decoupling, because it considers that remaining coupled payments have led to competitive distortions within the EU (Q 111, Q 118).[35] This view is shared by the German government, which is in favour of decoupling "all the premiums, because we need equal terms of competition for all Member States, especially in the animal sector where a lot of premiums are still coupled in other Member States" (Q 411). The Danish government too is in favour of further decoupling, even though it has maintained some partially coupled payments, because it considers that "the effects would not be very hard at this point in time because prices are what they are" (Q 445). Meanwhile Commissioner Mandelson was emphatic that production-linked subsidies must be left behind (Q 755).

107. Other witnesses were less enthusiastic about the Commission's proposals. COPA-COGECA's Secretary-General told us that his organisation had identified a number of sectors where production was expected to "more or less totally disappear because of the relatively high costs of production" if support was fully decoupled (Q 573). Echoing Commissioner Fischer Boel's views on the desirability of a diversified European agriculture industry, he argued that in order to maintain this, "we should have some sort of guarantee that we have the possibility to continue with particular products." The Scottish Cabinet Secretary for Rural Affairs was more conciliatory, recognising that legacy schemes should end, but stressing that some kind of flexibility for coupling would continue to be necessary (Appendix 4, Para. 18). He emphasised the need to protect at least part of the livestock sector—and notably the Scottish beef sector—if that sector, and the associated processing industry, were not to disappear. Mr Lochhead went on to suggest that national envelopes under Article 69 of the 2003 Regulation could offer a way of securing this aim.[36]

108. The Scottish NFU suggested that where there are strong reasons for retaining production—such as where cattle grazing preserves a landscape—"simple and effective measures" to achieve this aim should be introduced under Pillar 2 (Memorandum, Para. 4). The Scottish Executive and the French government, however, insisted that Pillar I was the most appropriate tool for maintaining agricultural activities in Less Favoured Areas (Appendix 4, Para. 19 and Q 506, respectively). The Commission warned that "we cannot introduce coupled payments into Pillar II because we would destroy the green value of Pillar II" in the WTO context , and that another solution must therefore be sought where the aim is to preserve livestock in a particular region (Q 694).

Conclusions

109. **We strongly support the Commission's proposal to eliminate partial coupling wherever possible. Coupled payments result in the misallocation of resources and distort both trade and competition. For those reasons, we consider that full decoupling in all sectors should be the ultimate objective of policy in this area. However, we recognise that progress towards this objective will require**

---

[35] NFU Cymru and NFU Scotland also support full decoupling.

[36] See also Para. 9 of this report.

considerable adjustment in some sectors. Article 69 funds could temporarily be used to facilitate such adjustment.

110. **While we accept that for social or environmental reasons, it may be considered desirable to sustain particular types of farming activity in fragile rural areas, we believe that such support should not be channelled exclusively through agriculture, but should instead be part of a broader rural development strategy delivered through Pillar II. Due to the need to preserve the WTO credentials of Pillar II, this implies that support for vulnerable rural areas should not be linked to particular types of production, but should instead directly target the desired environmental or economic externalities. An additional reason to avoid links to particular products is that as the effects of climate change set in, it may become increasingly expensive or altogether impossible to sustain traditional patterns of production.**

Set-Aside

111. The obligation on farmers to leave a certain proportion of arable land fallow or use it for non-agricultural purposes was introduced in order to reduce cereal production at a time when there were persistent surpluses. Market conditions have now changed dramatically, with rising demand pushing cereal prices up and creating a strong incentive to mobilise the land that has been kept out of production through the compulsory set-aside scheme.

Commission Proposals

112. The Commission consequently points out that "the need to limit supply seems to constrain the arable sector in the EU from the potential benefits of increased world market prices", and proposes to abolish compulsory set-aside.[37] As the compulsory rate of set-aside has already been set to zero, the practical effect of this proposal is to rule out the re-introduction of such controls in future sowing seasons.

113. The Commission does, however, caution that "the permanent abolition of set aside will require steps to preserve the environmental benefits accrued from the present scheme."[38] One possibility would be to "replace it by locally targeted rural development measures", it suggests.

Witnesses' Views

114. Most of our witnesses were in favour of the abolition of set-aside, on the principle that this supply management tool has outlived its purpose and prevents farmers from responding to market signals—the very principle behind the 2003 reform package (DEFRA, Q 37; NFU Q 122; Scottish Executive, Appendix 4, Para. 21; RSPB, Q 100). A representative response was that of Scottish NFU President Andy Robertson, who explained that "set-aside to us seems to be an anachronism now. In a decoupled era there should not really need to be some kind of artificial restraint on the extent to which people can grow crops" (Q 353).

115. Other witnesses were more cautious, but for different reasons. Although COPA-COGECA supported and indeed pressed for the zero set-aside rate,

---

[37] Commission MEMO/07/476, p.5.

[38] Commission Communication (2007) 722, Pa. 3.3.

we were told that it would not wish to see the system abolished altogether, "because it is one of the very few remaining market management tools" (Q 576). Environmental groups, by contrast, were concerned that the environmental benefits that had accidentally flowed from set-aside should not be lost. Natural England told us that they had "real concerns" about the environmental degradation that will flow from the decision to set the compulsory set-aside rate to zero (Q 142). Baroness Young told us that the Environment Agency too was "deeply worried" by the prospect (Q 187). The Agency anticipated that it would have "a huge environmental impact" (Q 200), and suggested that the Health Check should attend to the introduction of measures to replace the impact of set-aside (Q 204).

116. On behalf of DEFRA, Sonia Phippard assured us that while "there is a lot of anxiety around the removal of set-aside", its evidence suggests that in fact farmers "are taking some sensible decisions about productive and fallow land and leaving unproductive land fallow above and beyond compulsory set-aside, and by and large they choose as set-aside areas their least productive land" (Q 37). Anxieties that "instantly all those set-aside areas will be in full production" were therefore misplaced. DEFRA's assessment, she added, was that "there is not a major catastrophe about to happen."

117. Commissioner Fischer Boel identified a need to "make an attractive agri-environmental scheme that can take over the environmental benefits there have been from set-aside" (Q 719)—a view shared by NFU President Peter Kendall (Q 122). Tom Oliver of the Campaign to Protect Rural England also saw the need to "bring set-aside—whether rotational or permanent—which is of environmental value into environmental stewardship", and suggested that this would require more funds for such schemes, because set-aside would no longer be doing that job for us "by accident, as it were" (Q 265).

Conclusions

118. **Like many of our witnesses, we take the view that compulsory set-aside has no place in the market-driven framework of the reformed CAP. We consequently support the Commission's proposal to abolish compulsory set-aside for good.**

119. **We recognise that this could lead to the loss of the environmental benefits associated with set-aside—although we also note that both the scale of such benefits, and the likelihood that they will be lost, varies across farms. As with partial coupling, however, we believe that the environmental benefits that have now become set-aside's *raison d'être* should be targeted directly via Pillar II.**

Market Intervention

120. The CAP still harbours a number of market intervention instruments—such as quotas, intervention storage, price support and export refunds—that were originally designed to manage the supply of agricultural produce in light of prevailing demand.

Commission Proposals

121. In its Health Check Communication, the Commission suggests that a "reflection" on the future of these remaining "old CAP" instruments is needed, notably in light of the medium-term outlook for agricultural

commodity markets, which is especially favourable for cereals and dairy products. As part of this exercise, the Commission proposes to examine "whether the existing supply management tools serve any valid purpose now, or whether they simply slow down the ability of EU agriculture to respond to market signals."[39]

122. A full review of the cereals intervention system is already underway, while the maize and rye intervention systems have already been reformed. The Commission proposes to extend the reforms applied to the maize sector to other cereals, with the single exception of bread wheat. This would allow most cereals to find their natural price level, while continuing to provide safety-net support for bread wheat.[40] Commissioner Fischer Boel explained that the proposed exemption for bread wheat was the result of "anxieties in the public that bread is a fundamental product in agriculture or is a daily need for consumers" (Q 709).

123. With respect to milk quotas, the Commission proposes to prepare the ground for the expiry of the milk quota system in 2015 by gradually increasing quotas to create a "soft landing".[41] It argues that if nothing were done until the quota regime ends, efficient farmers would be prevented from meeting market demand, while inefficient farmers would face an abrupt loss of income in 2015. It anticipates that certain regions—especially but not exclusively mountainous ones—will face particular difficulties in maintaining production once prices fall. It proposes that support measures could be introduced under a revised Article 69 of the 2003 CAP regulation and/or through rural development measures.

Witnesses' Views

124. The demise of the cereals intervention system was warmly welcomed by the UK government, which is pressing for the "abolition of the intervention price system and all the associated policy instruments, including production quotas and storage aids" (DEFRA Memorandum, Para. 15). The NFU was also supportive of the Commission's proposals in this respect (Memorandum, Para. 18). Further down the food chain, the Food and Drink Federation told us that its members were looking for "market orientation which allows farmers to respond to market signals from the food industry and obviously ultimately from consumers" (Ruth Rawling, Q 817). Ms Rawling pointed out that "there are already market-based types of systems which help farmers cope with price volatility" and that in any case "quite a lot of the management of price is done through long-term contracts", which provide a certain amount of stability for farmers (Q 818). Heather Jenkins of Waitrose also drew our attention to the role that contracts could play in stabilising markets (Q 864).

125. Other witnesses urged varying degrees of caution. NFU Scotland proposed that options for weakening cereal intervention, without removing the system altogether, should be considered (Memorandum, Para.12). NFU Cymru saw a continued need for private storage aid "to provide short-term relief in exceptional circumstances" (Memorandum, Para. 13). Meanwhile the French government has made clear that in its view, the CAP should continue

---

[39] Commission Communication on the Health Check, Para. 3.1.

[40] Op. cit. Para. 3.2.

[41] Op. cit. Para. 3.4.

to stabilise markets in agricultural goods (Q 513). Yves Madre of the French Permanent Representation to the EU explained that the aim would not be "to avoid the variations but to be sure that tomorrow farmers will be able to deal with the variations and able to avoid very, very high prices or very, very low prices because that is not good for the industry or for farmers." Crisis management measures should, however, "be used in a very exceptional way" (Q 515).

126. The Scottish Rural Property and Business Association also saw a continued role for "emergency intervention", notably in the case of flooding or disease (John Don, Q 213). In those circumstances, Mr Don argued, "Europe and our own government should protect us to keep us in business for the long term". The Country Land and Business Association conceded that "we cannot expect to be bailed out without doing our own bit ourselves", but stressed that "there are some things which go beyond what we can do however good businessmen we are" (David Fursdon, Q 215). Referring to the US and Canada's intervention systems, his colleague Alan Buckwell suggested that "nobody has the right answers", but insisted that "sweeping it under the carpet will not work because volatility is increasing" and will continue to "increase with market liberalisation, not diminish."

127. In general, the Commission's intention to increase milk quotas gradually provoked less resistance. The NFU and NFU Scotland were both in favour of the gradual elimination of milk quotas (Memorandum Para. 19 and Memorandum Para. 12, respectively). The French government, we were told, was also "very open-minded" and intending to consider the Commission's proposal (Q 518). NFU Cymru and the FUW expressed concern about the way in which the transition would be managed (Memorandum, Para. 12 and Memorandum Para. 4, respectively). The Polish government was also more cautious, welcoming the proposed increase in milk quotas, but warning that the current favourable market context "is not the best time to make a final decision about the abolition and dismantling of the quota system" (Q 795).

Conclusions

128. **The principle that market forces should be allowed to determine production decisions is inconsistent with all types of market intervention and supply management. We consequently support the Commission's intention to reform the cereals intervention system and would urge that the same approach be extended to other sectors and for that matter, to bread wheat. Exceptions will in our view only serve to exacerbate distortions, by creating an incentive for producers to gravitate towards those commodities for which a safety-net remains in place.**

129. **For the same reasons, we welcome the Commission's intention gradually to increase milk quotas with a view to their eventual elimination. We agree that the areas worst affected by the removal of quotas may need targeted support, but are concerned that wherever possible, such support should not be linked to the production of specific commodities. During a transitional period, compensatory measures funded through Article 69 may be necessary. In the medium term, however, we favour the rural development route over the Article 69 route for such compensatory action.**

130. We recognize the distinctive risks to which the agriculture industry is exposed, and share the Commission's assessment that risk management deserves further attention in the Health Check. We return to this issue in the next Chapter.

Export Subsidies & Import Tariffs

131. Any reforms to market intervention instruments undertaken as part of the Health Check exercise will have implications for both the internal (EU) and external (world) markets for agricultural products. Import tariffs currently insulate the internal market in agricultural goods, regulating third country exporters' access to the EU market. Prices are thereby kept artificially high, as competition is restricted. The average agricultural tariff is currently around 20 per cent, with sensitive products incurring tariffs of 70 per cent or more.[42] Meanwhile one of the ways in which excess production in the internal market is cleared is by subsidising the export of those surpluses. This has the effect of depressing world prices for agricultural products, to the detriment of third-country producers.

Commission Proposals

132. In its Health Check Communication, the Commission has made clear that if some form of intervention system remains, it should not rely on subsidised sales—whether these are external (via export subsidies) or internal.[43]

133. As part of the Doha round of trade negotiations, the EU has committed itself to phasing out all export subsidies by 2013. If successful, the Doha round should also lead to reductions in import tariffs on agricultural products. These commitments, which would result in further liberalisation of trade in agricultural products, affect many of our witnesses' attitudes to the reforms that might flow from the Health Check.

Witnesses' Views

134. Although most of our witnesses had come to accept that export subsidies will be withdrawn and a number—notably the UK government—strongly support that commitment, some witnesses did express their unease at the prospect. Andy Robertson of the Scottish NFU warned of the impact of eliminating export subsidies on domestic markets, noting that EU producers who no longer receive export subsidies might instead sell into the internal market, including the UK, and "pull down the market" (Q 351). The Food and Drink Federation drew attention to the issue of sequencing, insisting that export refunds for Non-Annex 1 products[44] "should not be phased out until we have a level playing field" in terms of import tariffs—which result in EU food and drink manufacturers paying higher prices for raw materials than their competitors elsewhere in the world (Ruth Rawling, Q 824). "Once we are able to buy raw materials at the same price as everybody else then we do not need them", Ms Rawling suggested (Q 828). Her colleague Tim Innocent, who is also Head of Purchasing at Nestlé, explained that sugar is one of the company's key raw materials, and that even after the recent reform

---

[42] HM Treasury/DEFRA 'A Vision for the Common Agricultural Policy', Para. 1.18, December 2005.

[43] Commission Communication on the Health Check, Para.3.1.

[44] Value-added products produced with CAP agricultural raw materials that were not included in the list of agricultural products annexed to the Treaty of Rome and subsequent EU treaties.

of the sugar regime, the price of sugar in the EU is not expected to arrive at the world level, resulting in a discrepancy. He consequently argued that "to make us competitive with our confectionery products to export to the free market, to the world market, we do need to continue to see some form of export refund for processed products" (Q 825).

135. The Food and Drink Federation was broadly supportive of the EU's commitment to reduce import tariffs, explaining that "what we are supporting really is alignment of prices" (Q 827). Ms Rawling pointed to the recent decision to suspend import duties on grain temporarily in light of soaring demand, and suggested that this might "help people see that in fact there is no need to be quite so scared of some of this reduction of tariffs" (Q 827). Meanwhile Commissioner Mandelson told us that import tariffs needed to fall due to internal demand, as well as external pressure: "our demand for agricultural produce and food is outgrowing our ability and the capacity of the shrinking farm sector to provide for that. We need to import more because demand is growing", he insisted (Q 754).

136. Even among the FDF's own ranks, however, some members were uneasy at the prospect of cuts in import tariffs. Sugar producers—who are facing a cut of approximately 70 per cent in the import tariff applied to third-country sugar imports—viewed this as "extremely damaging for the remaining European producers" and are therefore pressing for sugar to be treated as a sensitive product, we were told (Q 832). The President of the Scottish NFU warned that "the real danger is on import tariffs" (Q 351). Taking the example of Brazilian beef, he argued that if tariffs were substantially reduced, "then obviously Brazilian beef becomes much cheaper and it will drag the market price down in this country very substantially and it will do severe harm to an industry which already is being paid a price which is well below what is needed to meet their costs of production." He insisted that "we run the risk of tariffs being dismantled and product coming in which is inferior and undercutting us."

137. The issue of perceived inferiority—in terms of production standards—of agricultural imports from outside the EU was raised by a number of witnesses.[45] The French government was most insistent in this regard. Yves Madre argued that "it is a question of us being fair and if we want very strict rules on our farmers on what they produce in the European Union I have some difficulty understanding why we should allow anything to be imported within the European Union" (Q 531). He argued that this was also a question of food safety: "we need to be sure that what is imported and what will be imported is safe", adding that "if it is safe and everybody has the same rules there are no problems." For these reasons, Andy Robertson of the Scottish NFU argued that it would be "irresponsible not to include production standards in WTO negotiations" (Q 352). Some Council delegations have also emphasised "the need to promote health and animal welfare standards at international level that are as exacting as Community standards."[46]

---

[45] See for example Q 807.

[46] Press Release 15333/07 on the Agriculture and Fisheries Council Meeting held in Brussels on 26–27 November 2007, p. 9.

BOX 6

SPS Standards Explained

Article 20 of the General Agreement on Tariffs and Trade (GATT) allows governments to place restrictions on trade in order to protect human, animal or plant life or health, provided they do not use such restrictions as disguised protectionism. A separate agreement on food safety and animal and plant health standards (the **Sanitary and Phytosanitary Measures Agreement** or **SPS**) sets out the basic rules.

It allows countries to set their own standards, but stipulates that such standards must be based on science, and should be applied only to the extent necessary to protect human, animal or plant life or health.

WTO members are encouraged to use international standards and guidelines where they exist. They may set SPS rules that result in higher standards and more trade restrictions, but only if there is scientific justification for doing so. The SPS Agreement also clarifies which factors should be taken into account in carrying out risk assessments.

The WTO itself does not set SPS standards and has made clear that it does not intend to.

138. Duncan Sinclair, Agriculture Manager at Waitrose, warned that production standards would be a "very difficult issue" on which to try and reach agreement, pointing to previous experience in the Uruguay Round of trade negotiations (Q 873). Baroness Young of Old Scone, Chief Executive of the Environment Agency, told us that "the business of consistent global standards is quite a difficult one", and that at least with regard to environmental standards, these were "only a small part" of what determines competitiveness (Q 195). Labour market costs, by contrast, "are probably the biggest single factor in terms of a level playing field", she suggested.

139. Commissioner Mandelson insisted that the obligations placed on EU producers "are designed to make them competitive", and are "going where the market is heading in any case" (Q 756). He anticipated that "we are going to produce quality products which people can absolutely rely on in health and other terms which will correspond to the sorts of high standards that European consumers, and people like European consumers, want to pay for." He suggested that the EU was "at that end of the market" and that in that sense, agriculture is no different from any other production sector in Europe. Commissioner Mandelson also dismissed concerns about the safety of imported agricultural produce, pointing out that "as tariffs go down and our markets open then other goods will come towards our markets, that is absolutely true, but they do not just pass freely into our markets because they have to get over the hurdle of our SPS[47] agreement" (Q 766). He also emphasized that third countries needed to know that if they were producing safely and supplying products that meet EU standards there would be no penalisation of their produce, "no artificially high SPS standards which will be a bar which is impossible for them to get over" (Q 759).

140. Some of our witnesses, however, were sceptical of the route EU producers were being asked go down. Dai Davies of the NFU Cymru explained that

---

[47] Sanitary and phytosanitary standards that cover food safety and animal and plant health.

while Welsh farmers have been trying to produce a branded product in an attempt to add value, "at the end of the day, the vast majority of products sold abroad are sold on a price basis", meaning that ultimately "it is only a small section of our production that we can sell in that way" (Q 352). On behalf of the Spanish government, Valentin Almansa de Lara also called for reflection "on this so-called quality European standard", suggesting that "consumers are not prepared to pay for it" (Q 551). Duncan Sinclair of Waitrose explained that "many consumers expect imported product to reach the exact same standards as we would have within the European Union and in a whole range of different sectors that is not the case" (Q 873). He suggested that the EU might therefore need to consider whether it should try to differentiate EU produce in the marketplace, for example through welfare labelling.

141. Professor Alan Buckwell of the Country Land and Business Association drew attention to the environmental consequences of agricultural trade liberalisation: "If Europe insists on having higher and higher environmental standards, as it is and as we support, and wants to liberalise trade and implicitly reduce its production, who does it think these additional imports are going to come from and with what environmental impacts?" (Q 208). On behalf of the New Zealand government, however, Murray Sherwin pointed out that "if you can take a product unsubsidised and deliver it into the market at a competitive price, you are unlikely to be embodying a lot more energy than the price that you are competing against; you simply cannot afford that" (Q 313). He consequently emphasised the need to ensure that these issues are considered not just in terms of food miles, but as part of "a broader greenhouse gas footprinting approach, which is much more on the full life cycle." Duncan Sinclair of Waitrose concurred on the need to look at the entire picture, "including inputs and production system" (Q 868).

Conclusions

142. **We commend the European Union's decision to commit itself to the removal of export subsidies, and strongly support the Commission's intention to ensure that subsidised sales do not form part of the CAP in future. We recognise the logic of the argument put to us by the Food and Drink Federation in respect of export subsidies for Non-Annex 1 products, but view it as a reason to cut import tariffs rather than keep export refunds.**

143. **The plight of manufacturers who use agricultural raw materials serves to highlight the broader redistributive impact of import tariffs, which protect producers of agricultural goods at the expense of consumers of those goods—be they households or large multinationals. In our view, this aspect of the CAP is without justification, and we therefore support further reductions in tariffs on all types of agricultural goods, including sensitive products. Current market conditions and the medium-term outlook for agricultural commodities[48] could, moreover, help to provide a soft landing for most sectors in the event of tariff reductions.**

---

[48] See for example the Food and Agriculture Organization of the United Nations' "Food Outlook", November 2007 and agribusiness consultants Bidwells' report on "The 'Bull Run' in Soft Commodities", October 2007.

144. **With respect to the production standards imposed on agricultural producers in the EU, we recognise the frustration felt by farmers who resent being exposed to competition while forced to observe rules that they regard as a competitive handicap. In our view, the demands placed on farmers are partly a consequence of the need to find a justification for the maintenance of direct subsidies. If direct payments are withdrawn and import tariffs reduced—as the UK Government advocates—then the production standards that EU producers of agricultural goods are obliged to respect should be re-examined. EU farmers might in future be asked to produce to SPS standards, with targeted financial incentives on offer through Pillar II for the provision of specific public benefits (e.g. high standards of animal welfare) that are not delivered by these production processes.**

145. **While supporting efforts to encourage other countries to adhere to production standards similar to those currently in force in the EU, we would not welcome attempts to impose such standards on other countries, nor the prospect of their being used as non-tariff barriers on imports. Agricultural products that meet the SPS standards stipulated by the EU should be allowed to enter. Consumers should then be allowed to choose among products produced to different standards above that basic threshold. Labelling will take on great importance if consumers are to make informed choices. Labelling should, however, be based on a comprehensive assessment of environmental impact and welfare standards, rather than relying on crude indicators such as whether a product has been air-freighted.**

CHAPTER 4: PILLAR II AFTER THE HEALTH CHECK

Modulation

146. Modulation is the mechanism whereby funds earmarked for Single Farm Payments in Pillar I can be diverted to fund rural development measures in Pillar II. The 2003 CAP reform made such transfers compulsory, fixing compulsory modulation rates of 3 per cent in 2005, 4 per cent in 2006 and 5 per cent from 2007 onwards until 2012.

Commission Proposals

147. In its Health Check Communication, the Commission identifies a number of new challenges which in its view require "a further strengthening of the second pillar".[49] It also draws attention to the constraints placed on Pillar II resources as a result of the 2005 budget deal, which saw substantial cuts to the funds allocated to rural development. The Commission points out that "with the CAP budget now fixed until 2013", rural development funds can only be topped up through "increased co-financed compulsory modulation." It therefore proposes to increase compulsory modulation by 2 per cent annually in budget years 2010 to 2013, so that compulsory modulation eventually reaches 13 per cent at the end of the financial perspective.

Witnesses' Views

148. The Agriculture Commissioner, Mariann Fischer Boel did not appear confident of securing Member States' agreement to this proposal. "If we manage to get through with plus eight [raising modulation from 5 to 13 per cent by 2013] then it would be one of the greatest victories we have ever had", she suggested. "It will be extremely difficult" (Q 699). The Commissioner also explained that she hoped to "agree with those countries that have introduced the voluntary modulation [that] they should reduce when we increase the compulsory modulation" (Q 686).

149. The latter aspect of the Commission's proposal addresses a concern raised repeatedly by farmers' unions in the UK. NFU President Peter Kendall argued that voluntary modulation places English farmers at a competitive disadvantage relative to their counterparts in other parts of the UK and other Member States, where voluntary modulation is either lower or not applied at all (NFU, Q 111). Dai Davies, President of the NFU Cymru indicated that his members too felt they were being "unfairly treated with regard to the imposition of voluntary modulation" (Q 323). Andy Robertson of the Scottish NFU pointed out that only the UK and Portugal apply voluntary modulation, "which means that in practice UK farmers and Portuguese farmers are having their direct support reduced to a level which is significantly below that for farmers in the rest of the EU" (Q 357).[50]

150. The farmers' unions were therefore broadly in favour of the Commission's proposal. Mr Davies told us he was very pleased that the Commission was proposing to match increases in compulsory modulation with decreases in

---

[49] Commission Communication on the Health Check, Para. 4.3.

[50] See also Mike Rumbles MSP, Appendix 5, Para. 1; John Scott MSP, Appendix 5, Paras. 3 and 4; and Sarah Boyack MSP, Para.3.

voluntary modulation (Q 323). Peter Kendall accepted that "uniform compulsory modulation is definitely preferable to [voluntary] national modulation" (NFU Q132). England's Regional Development Agencies also favoured compulsory modulation over voluntary modulation, on the grounds that the latter has "a distorting effect" (Q 399).

151. While welcoming increases in compulsory modulation, environmental groups were concerned that these should not be introduced in lieu of voluntary modulation. Natural England were looking for "an increase in compulsory modulation, but one which does not undermine voluntary modulation" because "50 per cent of the English requirement for agri-environment funds comes from voluntary modulation" (Q 142). The Royal Society for the Protection of Birds was hoping for modulation of up to 20 per cent, but wanted to "retain voluntary modulation as well" (Q 47).

152. Dr Phillips of Natural England identified a need to "get away from this mantra that high levels of voluntary modulation are some kind of English peculiarity" (Q 163). Responding to the argument that voluntary modulation introduces competitive distortions, she insisted that "it is not a level playing field; everyone has not started from the same place; there are a lot of historic accidents as to how funding is distributed; and I think that we need to accept the reality that different economies are in a position to move at different speeds" (Q 163). Meanwhile Alan Buckwell of the Country Land and Business Association explained that because under voluntary modulation "all the receipts remain in the Member states, that is more attractive from our perspective than compulsory modulation where 20 per cent of it is siphoned off" (Q 226).[51]

153. Professor Buckwell also drew our attention to a different problem, pointing out that "the UK is hoist by its decisions in the 1980s and 1990s to not make use of what we now call Pillar 2" (Q 226). Because the present allocation of rural development funds is based on historic allocations, the UK now has a "miserable" share of the Pillar II budget, Professor Buckwell observed. As a consequence, "if want to have sensible sized environment schemes and rural development schemes we have to modulate" (Q 226). Carmen Suarez of the NFU also noted that the historic distribution key "means basically that the UK gets very little, because the UK used to get very little" (Q 132). She emphasized the need to "ensure that there is a fair allocation of the resources of rural development funds", and suggested that if the allocation criterion were based on the percentage of land that is agricultural land, or the percentage of people living in rural areas, the UK would receive "a much fairer and definitely much higher allocation of rural development funds"(Q 132). Sonia Phippard of DEFRA agreed that having "a rural development share based on patterns of spend in the early Nineties will by 2010–2011 be completely ludicrous" (Q 23). Indeed the UK "would argue that it is fairly ludicrous now", she added.

---

[51] Note however, that the Commission has proposed that in the EU-15, the current redistribution key for modulated funds will only apply to the first 5 per cent of additional modulation. For the remaining 3 per cent, and for the 3 per cent applied in the new Member States, all the funds obtained from modulation will remain with the Member State in which they were generated. Commission MEMO/07/476, p.10.

Conclusions

154. **We support the Commission's plans to increase compulsory modulation, on the basis that funds invested in Pillar II of the CAP offer better value for the taxpayer than funds allocated to Pillar I. We share the view articulated by some of our witnesses that the high level of voluntary modulation applied by the UK can be traced back to its low share of rural development funds overall. If a historic allocation system for Single Farm Payments is considered indefensible—as the Commission has indicated, and as we believe—then a similar system for allocating rural development funds, based on a reference period even further in the past, cannot be justified. We therefore recommend that the distribution key for rural development funding be reviewed at the earliest opportunity.**

155. **In the meantime, we support the Commission's intention to secure like for like reductions in voluntary modulation in return for increases in compulsory modulation. We recognise that environmental groups in the UK rely heavily on funds from voluntary modulation to support their activities. In our view, however, the preservation of a level playing field across the Single Market in agricultural goods must be the overriding purpose of the CAP. We therefore share the farmers' unions' concern that the high levels of voluntary modulation being applied in the UK may result in competitive distortions.**

Risk Management

156. Farmers face two main types of risk: price risk, stemming from volatility in input or output prices; and production risk, stemming from disease, weather, etc. In the EU, price support instruments have traditionally protected farmers from some forms of price risk, while production risk has in some cases been mitigated by making compensation available, for example when animals are slaughtered to prevent the spread of disease. Since the implementation of the 2003 CAP reform, decoupled direct payments have substantially reduced the risks to which farmers are exposed by providing a fixed level of guaranteed income.

Commission Proposals

157. In its Health Check Communication, the Commission notes that changes in market instruments and the shift towards direct producer support have prompted discussion of different ways of managing risk.[52] It has in the past looked into the feasibility of an EU-wide risk management scheme, but concluded that "at least as long as intervention as a safety net continues", an EU-wide solution would not be appropriate. However, Community support for risk management has recently been introduced as part of reforms to the fruit and vegetable and wine regimes.[53]

---

[52] Commission Communication on the Health Check, Para. 4.1.

[53] The 2007 reform of the fruit and vegetable regime (Council Regulation 1182/2007 EC) offers Community financial support to producer organisations, which may engage in crisis prevention and crisis management measures (such as harvest insurance, training, or support for the administrative costs of setting up mutual funds). These measures are financed with operational funds that may be co-financed by the EU.

158. As part of the Health Check, the Commission wishes to encourage Member States, regions and producer groupings to devise their own tailor-made risk management measures under Pillar II of the CAP. It proposes to allow modulation receipts to be used for risk management measures, provided that they meet WTO green box criteria. It also intends to examine the need for additional measures should further adjustments to market mechanisms become necessary.

Witnesses' Views

159. A number of our witnesses were wary of where these proposals might be leading. Peter Mandelson, the EU Trade Commissioner, warned that he would be "a bit nervous of reform moving in that direction because we are starting to become close to the sorts of trade distorting programmes that the United States like to operate" (Q 753). Lord Rooker too was cautious, pointing out that "other businesses—non-farming, non-agricultural—have to take account of the risks of running their business" (Q 913). "We see it as no different for farms; so we are a bit suspicious of the concept of, let us say, a new scheme of risk management". While acknowledging that private insurance is not always available (Q 961), Lord Rooker insisted that risk management was "a matter for the industry, not for Brussels to come along and impose some scheme or some regime of risk-management" (Q 913).

160. Commissioner Fischer Boel assured us that the Commission's "ideas on risk and crisis management will always leave the responsibility to the farmer to tackle the normal risks that are in every business" (Q 721). She emphasised that "we do not want a European scheme for crisis management, we want Member States to create schemes, but we would be open to look at the possibility of co-financing the premium via the rural development scheme". She also addressed Mr Mandelson's concerns, warning that "if there should be any expectations of an income safety net, forget it". That, she argued "would be a countercyclical payment, exactly what we are accusing the Americans of using as the most trade distorting measure" and would not meet green box criteria. The Commissioner was adamant that "that simply will not fly" (QQ 721–724).

Conclusions

161. **We share the Government's view that risk management is a normal feature of any commercial activity, and should therefore take place within the industry to the maximum degree possible. However, we recognise that state intervention through the CAP over the years has impeded the development of industry-based solutions, and that private sector insurance and hedging instruments are not available in all sectors, nor necessarily adapted to the distinctive risks faced by farmers. As the agriculture sector becomes more market-oriented, and farmers are increasingly exposed to market risks, we therefore do see a role for the CAP in promoting the development of non-trade distorting, industry-based risk management methods. This may involve providing information (for example on the expected impact of climate change in a particular region), facilitating structural change (for example where risk is pooled through cooperatives, or through vertical integration in the supply chain), or co-financing insurance premiums as the Commission envisages—although the latter measure**

should in our view be time-limited rather than permanent. The ultimate aim would be to shift a greater share of market risk onto the agriculture industry. However, we recognise that the state is unlikely to be able to withdraw from this area altogether, notably where a private insurance market is unlikely to emerge—as may be the case with respect to risks posed by animal diseases or climate change, for example.

Climate Change, Bio-Energy, Water Management, Biodiversity

162. The agriculture sector is both a significant contributor to climate change, and a prominent victim of its effects. The sector is increasingly likely to face environmental challenges such as water scarcity and flooding, but is simultaneously under pressure to reduce its greenhouse gas emissions. The industry also has a central role to play in protecting biodiversity and in allowing the EU to meet its biofuel and renewable energy targets.

Commission Proposals

163. In its Health Check Communication, the Commission identifies climate change, bio-energy and water management as "three crucial new challenges for EU agriculture", with climate change as the pivotal one.[54] It notes that EU agriculture has contributed more than other sectors to the reduction of greenhouse gas emissions, but that it will be called on to curb its emissions further. The Commission also points out that the sector is highly exposed to climate change, and consequently identifies a need to improve adaptation practices. It predicts that targets for the share of biofuels (10 per cent) and renewable energy (20 per cent) in total fuel and energy consumption in 2020 are likely to have a significant impact on EU agriculture. The Commission notes too that the Health Check provides an opportunity to examine how water management issues can be integrated into the CAP, and recalls that biodiversity decline remains a major challenge.

164. Although existing provisions already allow all four issues to be addressed in rural development plans, the Commission outlines a range of policy adjustments that could be introduced as part of the Health Check. Rural development guidelines could be adapted to create stronger incentives for mitigating and adapting to climate change, for sustainable water management, for providing bio-energy services and for biodiversity protection. Alternatively, climate change and water management objectives could be incorporated into one or both elements of cross-compliance. The Commission regards research and innovation as "crucial" to these new challenges, and proposes that incentives for research into second-generation biofuels should be reinforced. It also announces its intention to examine whether the present support scheme for energy crops is still cost effective in light of new market incentives for biomass production.[55]

165. The Commission concludes that if measures to meet these challenges are to be effectively employed, further strengthening of Pillar 2 is essential.[56] It

---

[54] Op. cit. Para. 4.2.

[55] Commission Memo 07/476, p.8.

[56] Op. cit. p.9.

consequently calls for more financial resources for Pillar 2, to be obtained through an increase in compulsory modulation.[57]

Witnesses' Views: Mitigation

166. Commissioner Fischer Boel took the view that agriculture could do more to reduce its emissions from primary production, and that while possibilities already exist within the rural development scheme, "we need to reinforce the use of those possibilities" (Q 727). The English RDAs concurred on the need to create a stronger relationship between the climate change agenda and the principal environmental measures available to land managers, pointing out that existing environmental stewardship schemes in England did not address climate change issues but instead primarily addressed biodiversity issues (Q 371).

167. Poul Christoffersen, Head of the EU Agriculture Commissioner's Cabinet, pointed out that "the greenhouse problem from agriculture is not so much CO2 as the other types of greenhouse gases" (Q 727). NFU President Peter Kendall acknowledged this, explaining that "it is quite a new preoccupation to focus on methane emissions from cattle" and that the industry will "have to look at how we can vary diets; how we can change grazing patterns; whether we use different grasses" (Q 129). He called for more R&D spend to address these issues—a call echoed by the Danish and German governments. Kirsten Holm Svendsen of the Danish Permanent Representation to the EU suggested that Article 69 of the 2003 CAP Regulation could be used to fund innovation and research in this area (Q 451).

168. Natural England identified three ways of reducing emissions: "production methods with a lower greenhouse gas contribution; practices which encourage the retaining of carbon in soils; but, equally importantly, food prices that reflect the externalities" (Helen Phillips, Q 165). Dr Phillips suggested that improved management of peat soils in particular could be "a very cost effective way of going about carbon mitigation" (Q 164). Meanwhile Murray Sherwin of the New Zealand Government drew our attention to his country's intention to move to "a comprehensive emissions trading regime, which is all greenhouse gases in all sectors", including agriculture (Q 310). The agriculture sector, he explained, would be expected to start off "with an allocation of essentially free units, which will be scaled down over a period" (Q 312).

Witnesses' Views: Adaptation

169. Many witnesses pointed out that while climate change presented a challenge for the agriculture industry, it could also create new business opportunities and income streams for farmers.[58] Helen Phillips of Natural England suggested that agriculture would have "an absolutely and utterly unique role" to play in adapting to climate change (Q 164). She emphasized the need for sustainable practices; "for instance less use of fertilizers, more sensible use of agricultural wastes", and for preventive measures, such as the establishment of wildlife corridors allowing species and habitats to migrate. The RSPB anticipated that the industry would have to move to new crops and new ways of farming (Q 92).

---

[57] Commission Communication on the Health Check, Para. 4.3.

[58] See for example RSPB Q 56.

170. Some of these could prove lucrative. Fiona Bryant of the English Regional Development Agencies suggested that climate change adaptation should be regarded as a "huge opportunity, whether that is reducing CO_2 emissions through waste management, through addressing diffuse pollution, through providing renewable energy and a number of other areas of activity"(Q 370). She pointed out that although it had been anticipated that agriculture could provide ecological services, this had thus far been interpreted in terms of biodiversity. A much wider interpretation was required, encompassing the efficient use of resources and the potential use of carbon capture storage and sequestration. NFU President Peter Kendall also saw "big potential" in renewable energy, notably in new technologies, by-products and waste (Q 124). Walter Duebner of the German Permanent Representation confirmed that renewable resources "provide new income possibilities for farmers" (Q 427). He suggested these could become a "new production line" for farmers, who "do not depend on food production alone any longer, they have another outlet." Ian Baker of the English Regional Development Agencies cautioned, however, that these opportunities would "only be fully realised if farmers themselves are talking to other people in those same supply chains, and the people who essentially manage the markets where their produce is going" (Q 381).

Witnesses' Views: Biofuels

171. Commissioner Fischer Boel said that "we do not need the energy scheme that we have at present" (Q 727). She made the argument that "today we have a well-functioning market so I hope we can agree this will disappear and then maybe spend the money in innovation or the possibilities of developing the second generation of biofuels instead". Most of the evidence we received was implicitly supportive of the Commissioner's stance. Baroness Young of Old Scone, CEO of the Environment Agency, pointed out that "if we are moving away from funding production, we should not be helping fund biofuel production particularly" (Q 197). She went on to propose that the carbon market ought to fund biofuel production, by setting the right long-term price for carbon.

172. Many witnesses called into question the net environmental impact of first-generation biofuels. Baroness Young suggested that the biofuels target for Europe "clearly cannot be achieved within the European arable area, unless we put the whole area under biofuels" (Q 195). The Environment Agency, she explained, was "pretty sniffy about biofuels anyway, because we think that certainly first-generation biofuels are not exactly the most effective way of reducing carbon and that we need to move to second-generation biofuels" (Q 195). Natural England emphasized the need to "avoid production subsidies for biofuels, because with that, we will see all the things that we do not want, such as very big monocultures of biofuels" (Q 166). Murray Sherwin pointed out that "there are very few biofuel opportunities or options out there right now which are both economically and environmentally positive" (Q 317).

173. Some witnesses were equally concerned about biofuels imported from outside the EU to meet the biofuels target. The RSPB warned that "it would be bizarre if we cut down rainforest and create greenhouse gas emissions from doing that to create biofuels, some of which have a rather poor record themselves in saving greenhouse gas emissions, but that seems to be one direction we might be heading in" (Q 82). Baroness Young insisted that "if

we are to have a biofuels market globally, we do need to see some sort of accreditation process or certification scheme" (Q 195)—a call echoed by Natural England.

174. Sonia Phippard stressed the UK Government's "very firm view that as we look at the fuel alternatives, we need to be very, very clear both about looking for the most efficient sources of them, which may not be European, and at the environmental impacts of those sources" (Q 15). Baroness Young pointed out that if the aim was to identify the most environmentally effective and least environmentally damaging ways of impacting on carbon "the hierarchy would be energy from waste; energy from biomass; and biofuels coming quite a long way down after that—unless the second-generation biofuels really start to come through" (Q 197).

Witnesses' Views: Resources

175. The Agriculture Commissioner has presented the environmental challenges facing the agriculture sector as a justification for transferring resources from Pillar I to Pillar II. Mariann Fischer Boel pointed out to us that "the budget for agriculture will not be increasing after 2012. We will have lots of different challenges but we have not asked for more money. We will simply try to reallocate within our budget" (Q 731). Her Chef de Cabinet, Poul Christoffersen, likened this to an offer to fund climate change measures at no extra cost: "We are actually saying we are prepared to finance this by moving more money into the second pillar" (Q 729). "It would be difficult to find another financial donor", the Commissioner suggested (Q 729).

176. Her colleague Dalia Grybauskaite, the Budget Commissioner, was more optimistic, anticipating that other financial donors were likely to come forward, albeit with mixed motives. With reference to environmental challenges, she stressed the need "to avoid duplication", pointing out that "we have these elements in separate policies and they all fight, [saying] 'I need to do it', because they want to keep their portfolio" (Q 653). She consequently warned that "the creative minds in this house and outside are working very hard to keep things [resources] in the same pockets" (Q 675).

Conclusions

177. **We support the Commission's intention to review whether the strategic guidelines for rural development in the period 2007–2013 offer appropriate incentives for farmers and land managers to address the challenges and exploit the opportunities posed by climate change, including research and development, sustainable water management and the protection of biodiversity. We note, however, that because rural development programmes are drawn up by the Member States themselves, the onus is also on them to review whether their rural development and climate change agendas are suitably aligned. The Commission's review should therefore be complemented by equivalent reviews at the national level. Particular attention should be given to whether the right measure of flexibility is available to support measures that cut across the EAFRD axes, notably where there is both a business development and an environmental aspect to a particular project.[59]**

---

[59] On this point, see Q 378 of the oral evidence given by England's Regional Development Agencies.

178. **We would not support moves to incorporate climate change and water management objectives in cross-compliance. This would in our view add to the administrative burden faced by farmers, while duplicating policy objectives that are already addressed in Pillar II and in the Water Framework Directive.**

179. **We concur with the Agriculture Commissioner's verdict that market developments have removed the justification for subsidising biofuel production.[60] Production-linked subsidies run counter to the principle behind the 2003 CAP reform—support schemes for energy crops should be no exception.**

180. **We support the Commission's call for funds to be transferred from Pillar I to Pillar II so that adequate resources are available to implement the climate change agenda for agriculture. We note, however, the risk that the climate change agenda may be seized upon to resist calls for cuts to the overall CAP budget—a position that may be implicit in the evidence given to us by the Agriculture Commissioner.**

---

[60] This Committee has recently analysed the EU Strategy on Biofuels in its 47th Report of Session 2005–06, published on 20 November 2006.

CHAPTER 5: LOOKING AHEAD

The long-term future for Pillar I

Phasing out direct payments

181. The UK Government has made clear that between 2015 and 2020, it would like to see the "present Pillar I and all its works" fall away (Q 3 and Q 6). Lord Rooker explained that the UK views Pillar I as "money straight into the bank for no particular purpose whatsoever" (Q 879). Among its allies, Sonia Phippard of DEFRA told us, the UK counts the Swedish and Danish governments, and to a lesser extent, the German and Dutch governments (Q 5). Among the new Member States, the Estonian, Latvian, Maltese and Czech governments are seen as sympathetic. But Ms Phippard conceded that it is only the UK and Sweden "who have said unequivocally, with a timescale, that Pillar I payments should come to a complete end" (Q 7). The Danish government's policy towards the CAP is premised on a parliamentary decision calling for the eventual abolition of all direct support to farmers (Q 451). But Kirsten Holm Svendsen, Agriculture Counsellor at the Denmark's Permanent Representation to the EU, warned that this position came with strings attached, notably that Danish farmers be left "on an even footing" with competitors. She observed that this "explains why we work very hard for more trade liberalisation and getting rid of support everywhere else" (Q 452).

182. Among the Member States who wish to retain direct payments under Pillar I, France is "probably the most vocal", DEFRA told us (Q 10). Ireland, Luxembourg, Austria, Greece, Finland, Poland and Hungary are among France's allies in this respect (Q 10). Beniamin Gawlik of Poland's Permanent Representation to the EU confirmed that his government "would definitely like to retain the direct income support", adding that "for us, there is no room for discussion about the level of direct payments, especially as we are still waiting to get full direct payments" (Q 782). On behalf of the French government, Yves Madre warned that "Pillar II is useful, but we are afraid that Pillar II is not enough". He argued that "if we want to maintain agricultural activities the best tool is Pillar I" and insisted that "we need Pillar I and Pillar II" (Q 510). Closer to home, Scotland's Cabinet Secretary for Rural Affairs also saw a continued need for Pillar I support in the short- to medium-term (Appendix 4, Para. 23).

183. The introduction of an element of co-financing in Pillar I could be a half-way house between these two visions for the future of direct payments. The idea has been floated by the Dutch government among others (Q 19). The EU Budget Commissioner, Dalia Grybauskaite, made clear that she was open to the possibility, noting that 12 Member States—the most recent entrants—are already co-financing direct payments (Q 648). She warned, however, that this proposal was unlikely to be welcomed by those who benefited most from the current system, who would be asked to add something from their own budgets (Q 649). Ms Grybauskaite predicted that "the easy money which has been decided in the first pillar, especially now for the main beneficiaries and new Member States, is becoming more and more addictive. This will be a serious obstacle to reform" (Q 651).

184. For its part, the UK Government views co-financing as "something of red herring when it comes to Pillar I" (Q 19). It "does not seem to us that it is a particularly helpful step on the way to reducing Pillar I", a DEFRA official explained (Q 19). The official conceded, however, that co-financing "would certainly enhance Finance Ministries' interest in the cost, particularly Finance Ministries in the Member States who are net recipients rather than net contributors" (Q 21). Commissioner Fischer Boel told us that her "personal view on co-financing of the first pillar is that it is the first step to a total re-nationalisation of the Common Agricultural Policy" (Q 139). She warned that "if it was voluntary for Member States to co-finance I know two countries that would be very hesitant, the UK and Denmark, to co-finance one single cent. Then you would have no level playing field for European farmers anymore" (Q 688).[61]

185. Commissioner Grybauskaite pointed out that "rural development is co-financed, all structural actions are co-financed and 12 Member States' direct payments are co-financed until 2013 (until 2016 in the case of Bulgaria and Romania), so practically today we have the phenomenon of co-financing" (Q 647). "Is it renationalisation?", she asked. "We still call it the Common Agricultural Policy." She thus insisted that "it is not really about co-financing, it is if co-financing is voluntary that it is a problem ... if it is mandatory and you fix the exact amounts you equalise the conditions and the competition in all Member States" (Q 647).

Transferring funds to Pillar II

186. The desirability of transferring funds from Pillar I to Pillar II generated more consensus among our witnesses. The Agriculture Commissioner explained that "we need more money and, therefore, we want to increase the budget for rural development by reducing the direct payments" (Q 689). Her colleague Dalia Grybauskaite, the Budget Commissioner, appeared to be willing to transfer budget lines accordingly: "if we decide that rural development is a more progressive part of the policy, why not do what we want to without any modulation," she asked(Q 646). Meanwhile the UK Government maintains that Pillar II is "far better value" than Pillar I, and consequently hopes that "the pressure from that angle will be to bring Pillar I down while protecting, and indeed potentially enhancing, Pillar II (Q 6).

187. However, there was resistance in some quarters. Richard Lochhead, Scottish Cabinet Secretary for Rural Affairs pointed out many would question why money needed to be taken away from land managers and food producers in order to achieve the wider goals that are addressed in Pillar II (Appendix 4, Para. 30). Dalia Grybauskaite warned that Member States, "especially the newer ones, are less and less interested in the second pillar because it is more difficult to absorb, it is easier to go for the first pillar" (Q 664). Indeed even some old Member States appear to be wary of such moves. Walter Duebner of the German Permanent Representation to the EU pointed out that Germany's Eastern Länder do not have much money to co-finance Pillar II measures (Q 419). He explained their governments are consequently "very reluctant to have modulation or to spend even more money in the second pillar, they want to keep their money in the first pillar."

---

[61] Her concern was shared by the National Farmers' Union (Q 139).

188. A different note of caution was sounded by those who felt that some aspects of the CAP—and the associated budget lines—should be repatriated, rather than transferred to Pillar II. On behalf of the UK Government, Sonia Phippard argued that "we should not be either funding at a European level from a taxpayer point of view, or forcing through at a European level bureaucracy and inspection and enforcement of things that should be entirely down to Member State discretion" (Q 19). She concluded that "it is an entirely reasonable area to explore and really to work out what should be done at EU level and what should be done at national level." The Budget Commissioner, Dalia Grybauskaite, expressed similar concerns: "Can we afford to have a Common Agricultural Policy with such diversity between and inside Member States? That is a very fundamental question we need to ask" (Q 659). She too concluded that "what is possible and what can be done at a European level should be done at a European level, the rest should be given back." When asked what support she might garner for this proposition, Ms Grybauskaite identified "time, and only time" as her ally (Q 663).

189. Among those advocating the progressive reduction of Single Farm Payments under Pillar I, it was acknowledged that the environmental benefits currently delivered through the associated cross-compliance mechanism might need to be secured through a different channel. DEFRA made the distinction between the Statutory Management Requirements element of cross compliance, "which is simply obeying the law" and the "more obvious value added, the Good Agricultural and Environmental Condition" (Q 8). It appeared to envisage that the benefits delivered by the latter could be incorporated into the more ambitious entry-level Environmental Stewardship Scheme already in operation in England under Pillar II of the CAP (Q 8). In Scotland, environmental public goods are delivered through Rural Development Contracts (formerly Land Management Contracts), again under Pillar II. However, the Scottish Executive did not view Rural Development Contracts as a substitute for Pillar I in the long term (Appendix 4, Para. 15).

Conclusions

190. **The market and environmental objectives that we regard as the appropriate long-term aims of the CAP can in our view be pursued adequately with Pillar II instruments. We are therefore not convinced of the justification for maintaining direct payments under Pillar I in the long term. We would instead advocate a phased reduction in direct payments over the course of the next financial perspective. Periodic impact assessments should be used to determine the pace at which subsidies are withdrawn.**

191. **A significant proportion of the funds released by the progressive reduction in direct payments should in our view be transferred to Pillar II of the CAP for the duration of the next financial perspective, thus allowing for an orderly transition. While this course of action may not result in significant savings in the overall CAP budget, we consider it to be the only viable way of re-orienting the CAP, as it would avoid the upheaval involved in attempting to transfer budget lines and responsibilities away from the European Commission's DG Agriculture and national agriculture ministries.**

The long-term future for Pillar II

Purchasing Public Benefits—Land Management (EAFRD Axis 2)

192. The second facet of the UK Government's vision for the future of the Common Agricultural Policy is that once Pillar I has been eliminated, any remaining public subsidies should be "targeted at specific public benefits, such as environmental enhancement through Pillar II" (Lord Rooker, Q 875).

193. Our witnesses from the environmental sector presented very similar visions for the long-term future of the Common Agricultural Policy, which were broadly consistent with the principle endorsed by the UK Government. The Campaign to Protect Rural England called for the creation of an "Agricultural Public Benefits Fund" which would support the sustainable management of land for public benefit (Written Evidence, Para. 7). The Woodland Trust presented a very similar proposal (Written Evidence, Paras. 5 and 7). Meanwhile Natural England envisaged that the future of the CAP lay in paying farmers and other land mangers for forms of land management that maintain or restore environmental features that cannot be secured through the market or through advice and regulation alone (Written Evidence, Para. 3). The Environment Agency (Written Evidence, p.1) and the RSPB (Written Evidence, Para. 3) presented similar ideas.

194. The Country Land and Business Association advocated a more comprehensive approach, suggesting that the CAP should in future "incentivise land managers to produce the socially optimal qualities of high quality food and fibre, renewable energy, biodiversity, landscape, heritage, and soil, water and air management" (Written Evidence, Para.2). It also emphasised that "the environmental agenda for land management is larger than that of the agri-environment schemes, which is focussed mainly on landscape and biodiversity. Resource protections and maintenance, and climate change issues, for example, need to be given a higher priority." (Written Evidence, Para 9).

195. While subscribing to the principle that land managers should be rewarded for the public benefits that they provide, the UK farmers' unions felt that this principle provided a justification for continued direct payments under Pillar I, as the public goods that they were being called upon to provide are often inextricably linked to agricultural activity. The NFU Scotland, for example, argued that direct support would be "vital to keep farm businesses going, justified on the basis of paying for the 'non-market' goods that agriculture already delivers" (Written Evidence, Para. 6; see also NFU Q 107). On behalf of England's Regional Development Agencies, Fiona Bryant also made the point that "you need a sustainable business base to deliver those outcomes that they are looking for" (Q 379).

Business Development (EAFRD Axes 1 and 3)

196. The farmers' unions did see a role for Pillar II in providing support for business development. The Scottish NFU proposed that "a direct support payment should be complemented by business development measures as are currently available under Axis 1 of the Rural Development Regulation; and diversification measures as are currently available under Axis 3" (Written Evidence, Para. 7). It envisaged that these business development measures "would be aimed at helping farm businesses add value and reduce costs so

that profitability becomes less dependent on direct support." The NFU pointed out that "the UK seems to be out of kilter with other Member States when it comes to the allocation of rural development funds, and has decided to put much less money into competitiveness measures than other Member States" (Carmen Suarez, Q 132). Ms Suarez suggested that this was "probably something that we should call into question." The CLBA echoed this, proposing that greater emphasis be given "to the options under axis 1 and axis 3 [of the EAFRD] that provide support and assistance for improving the competitiveness and profitability of rural land-based businesses" (Written Evidence, Para 9).

197. England's Regional Development Agencies made a case for "mainstreaming" business development support for the agriculture sector. They pointed out that "many of the problems which farmers face are relevant to any business—managing change, improved marketing, adding value, risk planning and so on" (Written Evidence, Para. 16). In oral evidence, Ian Baker expressed the RDAs' belief that "some of the potential developments within the agricultural sector are being held back by the fact that farmers have historically regarded themselves as being separate and being provided with separate support" (Q 381). The RDAs suggested that by directing farmers to existing sources of assistance, they would be given the opportunity to access a wider range of business support mechanisms (e.g. Business Link), while also freeing funds to provide assistance to the wider rural economy (Written Evidence, Para 16).

198. The RDAs also pointed out that the support available under Axes 1 and 3 of England's Regional Development Plan is "very heavily focused on the farming sector" (Written Evidence, Para. 17). They warned that "any switch of funds from Pillar I to Pillar II needs to recognize the reality of the breadth of business interests now located on farms and the broader links to wider rural development."

199. However, there was strong resistance from the agriculture industry to the prospect of Pillar II funds being used to support rural development more generally. The Farmers' Union of Wales drew attention to an "increasing willingness by UK governments to divert Pillar II monies away from agriculture to a far greater extent than occurs in other Member States" (Written Evidence, Para. 5). Its members were of the opinion that "monies paid directly to farmers quickly filter down to other rural businesses while minimising unnecessary administrative costs." The NFU Cymru expressed concern that Pillar II rural development funding was "leaching away in favour of non-agricultural activity because of the minimum spends dictated by the EU under the various axes" (Written Evidence, Para. 17). It too made the argument that since agriculture remains the core activity in rural Wales, "allowing Pillar 2 resources to filter down to rural communities and businesses is a more efficient method of cascading down limited financial resources" (Written Evidence, Para 18). The Scottish NFU echoed these arguments (Written Evidence, Para. 13).

Rural Development (EAFRD Axis 3)

200. For its part, the UK Government has indicated that the CAP should in future include "a central rather than a peripheral role for rural development measures" (DEFRA Written Evidence, Para. 3). However, Lord Rooker emphasized that there was no question of relying solely on Pillar II to achieve

rural development objectives (Q 889), a point which received backing from England's RDAs. Ian Baker explained that "the social fabric [of rural areas] is something that requires investment from not just European but also state and local authority funds and by far the largest proportion is available through the local authorities" (Q 402). He consequently insisted that from the RDAs' perspective, "what comes through the national and European resources is really the icing on the cake." DEFRA made a similar argument with respect to the structural challenges facing the agriculture sector in the new Member States (Q 12).

201. The NFU was sceptical of the prospect of the CAP evolving into a rural development policy (Written Evidence, Para. 7). It pointed out that a common agricultural policy is required to prevent competitive distortions when farmers compete in an open single European market. "No such justification attaches to a common rural policy, any more than for a common urban policy", it argued. The NFU conceded that "there is, certainly, a need for a European policy framework to support under-developed regions, some of which may be rural", but insisted that "that is a different issue." On behalf of the French government, Yves Madre too warned that "we are not keen on financing with the CAP things that should be financed by the regional policy" (Q 520).

202. The NFU did, however, envisage a role for the CAP in regulating rural development policy, and drew attention to the distortions of competition that could arise from rural development programmes being run in other member states, alleging that some proposed programmes were close to being coupled support (Written Evidence, Para. 28).

Delivery

203. Although Lord Rooker indicated that the way Pillar II operates "is flexible enough and broad enough for us to deal with virtually all the objectives that we would want to deal with" (Q 887), DEFRA drew attention to problems with the practical implementation of rural development measures. It highlighted the "considerable amount of detailed information" that Member States must provide in order to get their rural development programmes approved by the Commission, and pointed out that the implementation and controls requirements "combine to provide a complex operating environment for Rural Development Programmes" (Written Evidence, Para. 19).

204. England's RDAs also lamented that whilst the EAFRD had drawn together a number of previously separate funds to improve the ability to set more strategic priorities, the finance and audit side appeared "to be based on the previously separate programmes, rather than following the integrated emphasis of the policy documents" (Written Evidence, Para 15). It concluded that the control and implementing measures had "done more damage to send those Axes back into their silos than was intended by the policy framework" (Fiona Bryant, Q 378). For example, projects have to be funded from one axis only and through one main measure, meaning that the added value of projects that cut across the axes may not be reflected in programme evaluation (Written Evidence, Para. 15).

205. Our attention was also drawn to the difficulties faced by those seeking to tap Pillar II support. The NFU Scotland called for a simplification of the application process for Pillar II schemes, too many of which require the input of professional consultants (Written Evidence, Para. 20). Lord Rooker too

noted that Pillar II schemes "are so complicated that people set up businesses to explain the schemes to people" (Q 887).

Conclusions

206. **Like the UK Government, we believe that the future of the CAP lies in the present Pillar II. A recast Pillar II could in our view form the basis for an EU-level framework for rural policy. For the reasons outlined by the NFU, the framework we envisage would not be a "common" rural policy in the sense of prescribing common solutions to common problems. Instead, the framework should specify a menu of actions that Pillar II funds can legitimately be used for. The main role for the EU would lie in defining the contents of that menu, ruling out measures that might lead to market distortions. Expenditure on R&D for example, might qualify for support, while countercyclical income safety nets would not. Each Member State would then be able to channel funds as it saw fit, in accordance with national priorities for rural development. We envisage that this system would differ from the existing policy framework in three main respects.**

207. **First, the types of admissible actions—currently organised around the three axes of the EAFRD—should in our view be recast more broadly to include more non-agricultural measures. Funds might thus be used to improve communications, infrastructure, and amenities in rural areas so as to ensure that rural communities are not disadvantaged by their rurality. The ultimate aim would be to ensure that non-agricultural economic activities are genuinely available and viable as the agriculture sector adapts and restructures in response to market signals. However, investment designed to improve the competitiveness of farming businesses should continue, and will become even more critical if agricultural trade is liberalised further.**

208. **Second, there should be no prescriptions for fixed percentages of Pillar II funding to be spent on different types of actions. Regulation at the EU-level should be limited to identifying the types of actions that are admissible, based on whether they might interfere with the operation of the Single Market.**

209. **Lastly, the distribution key for Pillar II funds should in our view be reassessed. We have already recommended that the current historical allocation system should be reviewed at the earliest opportunity. We believe that an element of co-financing should be preserved, as it provides Member States with incentives to ensure that funds are spent efficiently. Co-financing requirements should, however, be determined on a needs basis, so that a smaller proportion of co-financing is required from poorer Member States.[62] This will become particularly important if Pillar I funds are progressively transferred to Pillar II. Co-financing should nevertheless continue to be compulsory, in order to prevent distortions of competition.**

210. **A recast Pillar II such as we have described could in our view be used to tackle the relative deprivation of rural areas compared to urban areas even in relatively rich Member States, and to target pockets of**

---

[62] A similar principle already applies to convergence regions (those that are under-developed in relative terms), where EAFRD actions require a smaller percentage of Member State co-financing.

deprivation in otherwise wealthy rural areas—needs that are overlooked by other EU policies that allocate funds on the basis of absolute and average measures of deprivation. In practice, this would mean that all Member States would continue to benefit from access to CAP funds. Rather than duplicating what is being carried out through other EU programmes and funds—notably Structural and Cohesion Funds—the framework we have outlined should therefore close a gap exposed by these existing programmes.

CHAPTER 6: SUMMARY OF CONCLUSIONS AND RECOMMENDATIONS

The Purpose of the CAP post-2013

Economic Goals

211. We share our witnesses' view that the "commonality" of the CAP should be its central feature. The regulation of the Single Market in agricultural commodities within the EU should therefore continue to be the primary role of a Common Agricultural Policy. However, we also note that there is a difficult balancing act to be struck between preserving the "commonality" of the CAP and responding to calls for greater flexibility in the way common goals are delivered in different Member States and indeed in different regions within each Member State (see Para. 37).

212. We believe that the drive towards a more market-oriented agriculture should continue. In the long term, the CAP should aim to foster a farming sector that is capable of standing on its own feet, competing in open international markets without subsidy or special protection. We acknowledge the likelihood of greater demand for agricultural commodities in future, and believe that this presents an opportunity for the European farming industry. The distorting effect of subsidies will in our view hinder the EU agriculture sector's ability to respond to, and profit from, the expected increase in global demand for agricultural products. The CAP should instead aim to steer the industry towards a position from which it can take full advantage of a future boom in commodities prices. In our view, this means moving away from the distortions that a managed and protected internal market for agricultural commodities creates and sustains (see Para. 48).

213. We were not persuaded by the argument that the risk of future food shortages should be hedged against by freezing current production patterns. In our judgement, food scarcity is likely to be a function of income rather than of production capacity. If the supply shortages anticipated by some witnesses do materialise, those most at risk are consumers on low incomes in the developing world (see Para. 49).

Social Goals

214. We recognize that many Member States are currently relying on CAP funds—and particularly on direct payments under Pillar I—to secure social policy goals. However, we believe that many of the problems being addressed—such as the lack of employment opportunities in remote rural areas, or the fragility of rural communities—deserve to be tackled in their own right. Direct payments to farmers and landowners are an indirect, and in our view poorly-focused, instrument with which to address these challenges. Agricultural interests should not be equated with rural interests: channelling financial support through the agriculture sector may not be the most efficient and effective way of sustaining rural communities (see Para. 58).

215. The needs of rural communities are likely to be very different across different Member States and across different regions within each country. Agriculture may or may not have a role to play in meeting those needs, and different Member States will wish to give varying levels of prominence to the

agriculture sector in their overall rural development strategy. For this reason too, we consider that uniform direct payments to farmers under Pillar I of the CAP are not the appropriate vehicle for the implementation of a diverse set of national rural policies (see Para. 59).

216. We believe that some of these goals—such as the diversification of the rural economy—would be better pursued through Pillar II of the CAP (and indeed provision is already made for such actions under the EAFRD), while others—such as the structural problems in the rural areas of the new Member States—would be better tackled through other EU programmes (e.g. Structural and Cohesion Funds). Social and cultural objectives, however, are in our view too numerous and too diverse to be pursued exclusively through EU-level programmes. They should be addressed primarily at a national, or even sub-national level, at domestic taxpayers' expense (see Para. 60).

Environmental Goals

217. We recognize that certain types of farming activity can generate environmental benefits that are valued by society at large but whose value is not reflected in market prices for agricultural products. It does not automatically follow, however, that farmers should receive financial rewards for the environmental public goods that their activity helps to provide (see Para. 65).

218. We believe that the CAP should continue to promote farming methods and practices that will result in environmental benefits. In light of limited public resources, we see merit in drawing a distinction between environmental outcomes that can be secured through regulation—such as the control of emissions and pollution—and those that are unlikely to be delivered without financial incentives—such as the positive management of a wildlife habitat (see Para. 71).

219. We recognise the inherent difficulty in determining which environmental goods and services should be paid for from the public purse, and in putting a price on their value to society. We expect that these valuations may change over time, notably in the event of food price inflation. We consequently recommend that these decisions should be taken at a national level wherever possible, albeit on the basis of a menu of admissible uses for CAP funds defined at the EU level (see Para.73).

220. Climate change considerations will clearly have to figure prominently among the future environmental objectives of the CAP. The EU's agriculture sector will need to improve its impact on the environment, but climate change also presents a business opportunity for the industry, which it must be encouraged to seize. In the long run, the best way to secure progress towards both goals may be to integrate agriculture in an EU-wide greenhouse gas emissions trading scheme. We consequently recommend that this possibility be given further consideration as a matter of urgency (see Para. 75).

Pillar I after the Health Check

Basis for Single Farm Payments

221. The logic of the Commission's argument for moving away from historic payment models is compelling, and we therefore support its proposal to

encourage Member States to move towards a 'flatter' and, in our view, more rational and transparent payments system. We note that the language used by the Commission is permissive, and that it intends to allow Member States to decide "whether to move to flatter rates, at which scale (Member State-wide, regional ...) and to which extent." We believe that this very substantial degree of flexibility should go some way towards meeting the concerns raised (see Para. 81).

222. In the longer term, however, we are not convinced of the justification for maintaining direct payments under Pillar I, as the market and environmental objectives that we regard as the appropriate long-term aims of the CAP can in our view be pursued adequately with the instruments available under Pillar II. We therefore recommend that a progressive flattening of payments systems in the aftermath of the Health Check should in due course be accompanied by a phased reduction in direct payments over the course of the next Financial Perspective (see Para. 82).

Upper and Lower Limits for Direct Payments

223. While we understand the Commission's desire to bring about a fairer distribution of subsidies by tapering off subsidies at the top end, this approach rests on an implicit assumption about what the purpose of the CAP should be that we do not share. If the Common Agricultural Policy is to target social goals—and among them, a fair income for farmers—it might indeed make sense to set up a fair, and possibly even means-tested, system of allocating subsidies. But if as we have argued, the CAP should aim to promote a competitive, market-oriented agriculture industry, then it does not make sense to introduce a measure that will penalize those who undertake the restructuring that efficiency may require. We therefore do not support the introduction of thresholds above which subsidies are progressively reduced (see Para. 89).

224. By contrast, we do support the introduction of minimum thresholds for payments, as we are persuaded by the Commission's argument that it makes no sense to create subsidy entitlements that cost more to administer than the amounts being awarded. If Member States are given the flexibility to set their own minimum thresholds in the context of the structure of their farming industry, the new Member States will not be penalized (see Para. 90).

Cross Compliance

225. We welcome the Commission's intention to review the scope of cross-compliance by examining and amending the list of SMR and GAEC requirements. The evidence we have received suggests that while cross compliance has helped to deliver environmental benefits, and has been valuable in raising awareness of environmental issues among land managers, the administrative obligations associated with the regime are in some instances out of proportion to the benefits delivered. We therefore recommend that the Commission should focus on withdrawing elements from the current list of cross compliance conditions, rather than adding to it (see Para. 101).

226. This is not a task for the Commission alone: Member States too need to consider whether they are trying to pack too much into cross compliance, as this is not only likely to reduce the effectiveness of the tool and sap morale among land managers, but may also lead to competitive distortions.

However, we recognise that while Pillar I continues to absorb such a significant proportion of CAP spending, the environmental benefits delivered by cross compliance are an important part of the justification for public expenditure on direct payments (see Para. 102).

227. In the medium term, we believe that it would be appropriate to consider whether the SMR element of cross compliance needs to be included at all. We were persuaded in this respect by Natural England's contention that financial incentives should be guarded closely, and offered only in return for environmental practices that go over and beyond what is required by law—a criterion that Statutory Management Requirements fall foul of. The lever that cross compliance offers might therefore be used more sparingly, but to better effect (see Para. 103).

Decoupling

228. We strongly support the Commission's proposal to eliminate partial coupling wherever possible. Coupled payments result in the misallocation of resources and distort both trade and competition. For those reasons, we consider that full decoupling in all sectors should be the ultimate objective of policy in this area. However, we recognise that progress towards this objective will require considerable adjustment in some sectors. Article 69 funds could temporarily be used to facilitate such adjustment (see Para. 109).

229. While we accept that for social or environmental reasons, it may be considered desirable to sustain particular types of farming activity in fragile rural areas, we believe that such support should not be channelled exclusively through agriculture, but should instead be part of a broader rural development strategy delivered through Pillar 2. Due to the need to preserve the WTO credentials of Pillar 2, this implies that support for vulnerable rural areas should not be linked to particular types of production, but should instead directly target the desired environmental or economic externalities. An additional reason to avoid links to particular products is that as the effects of climate change set in, it may become increasingly expensive or altogether impossible to sustain traditional patterns of production (see Para. 110).

Set-Aside

230. Like many of our witnesses, we take the view that compulsory set-aside has no place in the market-driven framework of the reformed CAP. We consequently support the Commission's proposal to abolish compulsory set-aside for good (see Para. 118).

231. We recognise that this could lead to the loss of the environmental benefits associated with set-aside—although we also note that both the scale of such benefits, and the likelihood that they will be lost, varies across farms. As with partial coupling, however, we believe that the environmental benefits that have now become set-aside's *raison d'être* should be targeted directly via Pillar II (see Para. 119).

Market Intervention

232. The principle that market forces should be allowed to determine production decisions is inconsistent with all types of market intervention and supply management. We consequently support the Commission's intention to reform the cereals intervention system and would urge that the same

approach be extended to bread wheat and to other sectors. Exceptions will in our view only serve to exacerbate distortions, by creating an incentive for producers to gravitate towards those commodities for which a safety-net remains in place (see Para. 128).

233. For the same reasons, we welcome the Commission's intention to gradually increase milk quotas with a view to their eventual elimination. We agree that the areas worst affected by the removal of quotas may need targeted support, but are concerned that wherever possible, such support should not be linked to the production of specific commodities. During a transitional period, compensatory measures funded through Article 69 may be necessary. In the medium term, however, we favour the rural development route over the Article 69 route for such compensatory action (see Para. 129).

Export Subsidies & Import Tariffs

234. We commend the European Union's decision to commit itself to the removal of export subsidies, and strongly support the Commission's intention to ensure that subsidised sales do not form part of the CAP in future. We recognise the logic of the argument put to us by the Food and Drink Federation in respect of export subsidies for Non-Annex 1 products, but view it as a reason to cut import tariffs rather than keep export refunds (see Para. 142).

235. The plight of manufacturers who use agricultural raw materials serves to highlight the broader redistributive impact of import tariffs, which protect producers of agricultural goods at the expense of consumers of those goods— be they households or large multinationals. In our view, this aspect of the CAP is without justification, and we therefore support further reductions in tariffs on all types of agricultural goods, including sensitive products. Current market conditions and the medium-term outlook for agricultural commodities could, moreover, help to provide a soft landing for most sectors in the event of tariff reductions (see Para. 143).

236. With respect to the production standards imposed on agricultural producers in the EU, we recognise the frustration felt by farmers who resent being exposed to competition while forced to observe rules that they regard as a competitive handicap. In our view, the demands placed on farmers are partly a consequence of the need to find a justification for the maintenance of direct subsidies. If direct payments are withdrawn and import tariffs reduced—as the UK Government advocates—then the production standards that EU producers of agricultural goods are obliged to respect should be re-examined. EU farmers might in future be asked to produce to SPS standards, with targeted financial incentives on offer through Pillar II for the provision of specific public benefits (e.g. high standards of animal welfare) that are not delivered by these production processes (see Para. 144).

237. While supporting efforts to encourage other countries to adhere to production standards similar to those currently in force in the EU, we would not welcome attempts to impose such standards on other countries, nor the prospect of their being used as non-tariff barriers on imports. Agricultural products that meet the SPS standards stipulated by the EU should be allowed to enter. Consumers should then be allowed to choose among products produced to different standards above that basic threshold. Labelling will take on great importance if consumers are to make informed choices. Labelling should, however, be based on a comprehensive assessment

of environmental impact and welfare standards, rather than relying on crude indicators such as whether a product has been air-freighted (see Para. 145).

Pillar II after the Health Check

Modulation

238. We support the Commission's plans to increase compulsory modulation, on the basis that funds invested in Pillar II of the CAP offer better value for the taxpayer than funds allocated to Pillar I. We share the view articulated by some of our witnesses that the high level of voluntary modulation applied by the UK can be traced back to its low share of rural development funds overall. If a historic allocation system for Single Farm Payments is considered indefensible—as the Commission has indicated, and as we believe—then a similar system for allocating rural development funds, based on a reference period even further in the past, cannot be justified. We therefore recommend that the distribution key for rural development funding be reviewed at the earliest opportunity (see Para. 154).

239. In the meantime, we support the Commission's intention to secure like for like reductions in voluntary modulation in return for increases in compulsory modulation. We recognise that environmental groups in the UK rely heavily on funds from voluntary modulation to support their activities. In our view, however, the preservation of a level playing field across the Single Market in agricultural goods must be the overriding purpose of the CAP. We therefore share the farmers' unions' concern that the high levels of voluntary modulation being applied in the UK may result in competitive distortions (see Para. 155).

Risk Management

240. We share the UK Government's view that risk management is a normal feature of any commercial activity, and should therefore take place within the industry to the maximum degree possible. However, we recognise that state intervention through the CAP over the years has impeded the development of industry-based solutions, and that private sector insurance and hedging instruments are not available in all sectors, nor necessarily adapted to the distinctive risks faced by farmers. As the agriculture sector becomes more market-oriented, and farmers are increasingly exposed to market risks, we therefore do see a role for the CAP in promoting the development of non-trade distorting, industry-based risk management methods. This may involve providing information (for example on the expected impact of climate change in a particular region), facilitating structural change (for example where risk is pooled through cooperatives, or through vertical integration in the supply chain), or co-financing insurance premiums as the Commission envisages—although the latter measure should in our view be time-limited rather than permanent. The ultimate aim would be to shift a greater share of market risk onto the agriculture industry. However, we recognise that the state is unlikely to be able to withdraw from this area altogether, notably where a private insurance market is unlikely to emerge—as may be the case with respect to risks posed by animal diseases or climate change, for example (see Para. 161).

Climate Change, Bio-Energy, Water Management, Biodiversity

241. We support the Commission's intention to review whether the strategic guidelines for rural development in the period 2007–2013 offer appropriate

incentives for farmers and land managers to address the challenges and exploit the opportunities posed by climate change, including research and development, sustainable water management and the protection of biodiversity. We note, however, that because rural development programmes are drawn up by the Member States themselves, the onus is also on them to review whether their rural development and climate change agendas are suitably aligned. The Commission's review should therefore be complemented by equivalent reviews at the national level. Particular attention should be given to whether the right measure of flexibility is available to support measures that cut across the EAFRD axes, notably where there is both a business development and an environmental aspect to a particular project (see Para. 177).

242. We would not support moves to incorporate climate change and water management objectives in cross-compliance. This would in our view add to the administrative burden faced by farmers, while duplicating policy objectives that are already addressed in Pillar II and in the Water Framework Directive (see Para. 178).

243. We concur with the Agriculture Commissioner's verdict that market developments have removed the justification for subsidising biofuel production. Production-linked subsidies run counter to the principle behind the 2003 CAP reform—support schemes for energy crops should be no exception (see Para. 179).

244. We support the Commission's call for funds to be transferred from Pillar I to Pillar II so that adequate resources are available to implement the climate change agenda for agriculture. We note, however, the risk that the climate change agenda may be seized upon to resist calls for cuts to the overall CAP budget—a position that may be implicit in the evidence given to us by the Agriculture Commissioner (see Para. 180).

Looking Ahead

The long-term future for Pillar I

245. The market and environmental objectives that we regard as the appropriate long-term aims of the CAP can in our view be pursued adequately with Pillar II instruments. We are therefore not convinced of the justification for maintaining direct payments under Pillar I in the long term. We would instead advocate a phased reduction in direct payments over the course of the next financial perspective. Periodic impact assessments should be used to determine the pace at which subsidies are withdrawn (see Para. 190).

246. A significant proportion of the funds released by the progressive reduction in direct payments should in our view be transferred to Pillar II of the CAP for the duration of the next financial perspective, thus allowing for an orderly transition. While this course of action may not result in significant savings in the overall CAP budget, we consider it to be the only viable way of re-orienting the CAP, as it would avoid the upheaval involved in attempting to transfer budget lines and responsibilities away from the European Commission's DG Agriculture and national agriculture ministries (see Para. 191).

The long-term future for Pillar II

247. Like the UK Government, we believe that the future of the CAP lies in the present Pillar II. A recast Pillar II could in our view form the basis for an EU-level framework for rural policy. For the reasons outlined by the NFU, the framework we envisage would not be a "common" rural policy in the sense of prescribing common solutions to common problems. Instead, the framework should specify a menu of actions that Pillar II funds can legitimately be used for. The main role for the EU would lie in defining the contents of that menu, ruling out measures that might lead to market distortions. Expenditure on R&D for example, might qualify for support, while countercyclical income safety nets would not. Each Member State would then be able to channel funds as it saw fit, in accordance with national priorities for rural development. We envisage that this system would differ from the existing policy framework in three main respects (see Para. 206).

248. First, the types of admissible actions—currently organised around the three axes of the EAFRD—should in our view be recast more broadly to include more non-agricultural measures. Funds might thus be used to improve communications, infrastructure, and amenities in rural areas so as to ensure that rural communities are not disadvantaged by their rurality. The ultimate aim would be to ensure that non-agricultural economic activities are genuinely available and viable as the agriculture sector adapts and restructures in response to market signals. However, investment designed to improve the competitiveness of farming businesses should continue, and will become even more critical if agricultural trade is liberalised further (see Para. 207).

249. Second, there should be no prescriptions for fixed percentages of Pillar II funding to be spent on different types of actions. Regulation at the EU-level should be limited to identifying the types of actions that are admissible, based on whether they might interfere with the operation of the Single Market (see Para. 208).

250. Lastly, the distribution key for Pillar II funds should in our view be reassessed. We have already recommended that the current historical allocation system should be reviewed at the earliest opportunity. We believe that an element of co-financing should be preserved, as it provides Member States with incentives to ensure that funds are spent efficiently. Co-financing requirements should, however, be determined on a needs basis, so that a smaller proportion of co-financing is required from poorer Member States. This will become particularly important if Pillar I funds are progressively transferred to Pillar II. Co-financing should nevertheless continue to be compulsory, in order to prevent distortions of competition (see Para. 209).

251. A recast Pillar II such as we have described could in our view be used to tackle the relative deprivation of rural areas compared to urban areas even in relatively rich Member States, and to target pockets of deprivation in otherwise wealthy rural areas—needs that are overlooked by other EU policies that allocate funds on the basis of absolute and average measures of deprivation. In practice, this would mean that all Member States would continue to benefit from access to CAP funds. Rather than duplicating what is being carried out through other EU programmes and funds—notably Structural and Cohesion Funds—the framework we have outlined should therefore close a gap exposed by these existing programmes (see Para. 210).

APPENDIX 1: SUB-COMMITTEE D (ENVIRONMENT AND AGRICULTURE)

The members of the Sub-Committee which conducted this inquiry were:-

Earl of Arran
Lord Bach (up to 10 November 2007)
Lord Brooke of Alverthorpe
Viscount Brookeborough
Lord Cameron of Dillington
Earl of Dundee
Lord Greaves
Baroness Jones of Whitchurch
Baroness Miller of Chilthorne Domer (up to 9 November 2007)
Lord Moynihan (up to 10 November 2007)
Lord Palmer
Lord Plumb
Lord Sewel (Chairman)
Baroness Sharp of Guildford
Viscount Ullswater

Declarations of Interests Relevant to this Inquiry

Earl of Arran

The Earl of Arran's wife is a farmer in Devon
Trustee of certain family trusts associated with farming

Viscount Brookeborough

Farms in Northern Ireland and has in the past received an EU grant for diversification
Runs a farm-based tourist business

Lord Cameron of Dillington

Farmer and Landowner with commercial property interests in the countryside
Member of the National Farmers' Union
Member of the Country Land and Business Association
Member of the Campaign to Protect Rural England
Member of the National Trust
Member of the Council of the Royal Bath and West Society

Earl of Dundee

Farmer and owner of farmland and forestry
Director of farming company in Scotland

Lord Palmer

Member of the National Farmers' Union Scotland
Member of the Scottish Rural Property and Business Association
Farmer (in receipt of Single Farm Payment and other Rural Stewardship Scheme payments)
President of British Association for Bio Fuels and Oils
President of Transport Division of the Renewable Energy Association
Residual beneficiary of banana-growing estate in West Indies
Involved in rural tourism

Lord Plumb

Farmer and property owner in Warwickshire
Member of the National Farmers' Union
Member of the Country Land and Business Association

President of the National Sheep Association
President of the Royal Agricultural Benevolent Institute
President of the International Training Programme
Past President and Member of the International Policy Council on Food, Agriculture and Trade
Hon Trustee of the Royal Agricultural Society of England
Fellow of the Duchy College, Cornwall and the Royal Agricultural College, Cirencester
Former Master of the Worshipful Company of Farmers

Lord Sewel

No relevant interests

Viscount Ullswater

Director of farming company in Cumbria (Directors Fees)
Trustee of landed estates in Cumbria and Devon (Expenses)
Member of the Country Land and Business Association

APPENDIX 2: LIST OF WITNESSES

The following witnesses gave evidence. Those marked * gave oral evidence.

Agricultural Law Association

* Mr. Valentin Almansa de Lara, Agriculture Counsellor, Spanish Permanent Representation to the EU

Australian Government

Biscuit Cake Chocolate and Confectionery Association

* Mr. Reimer Boege, Member of the European Parliament, Chairman of the European Parliament's Budget Committee

Mr. Andrew Brown

* Campaign to Protect Rural England

* COPA-COGECA

* Country Land and Business Association

Countryside Council for Wales

Dairy UK

Ms. Sophia M. Davidova, Reader, Kent Business School, University of Kent at Wye College

* Department for Environment, Food and Rural Affairs

* Mr. Walter Duebner, Head of Agriculture, German Permanent Representation to the EU

* England's Regional Development Agencies

* Environment Agency

EuroChoices

European Commission

* Ms. Mariann Fischer Boel, European Commissioner for Agriculture and Rural Development

* Ms. Dalia Grybauskaite, European Commissioner for Financial Programming and Budget

* Mr. Peter Mandelson, European Commissioner for Trade

Family Farmers' Association

* Farmers' Union of Wales

* Food and Drink Federation

Food Ethics Council

* Mr. Beniamin Gawlik, First Secretary (Agriculture), Polish Permanent Mission to the EU

Professor David Harvey

Berkley Hill, Professor Emeritus of Policy Analysis, Imperial College London

Institute of Agricultural Management and Bidwells

Institute for European Environmental Policy

Ms. Sonia Kurta

Mr. W. H. Locker

★   Mr. Yves Madre, Delegate for European Agricultural Affairs, French Permanent Representation to the EU

Meat and Livestock Commission

★   National Farmers' Union of England and Wales

★   Natural England

The Rt. Rvd. John Oliver

★   New Zealand Government

★   NFU Cymru

★   NFU Scotland

★   Mr. Neil Parish, Member of the European Parliament, Chairman of the European Parliament's Agriculture Committee

Royal Agricultural Society of England

Royal Society for the Prevention of Cruelty to Animals

★   Royal Society for the Protection of Birds

Scottish Crofting Foundation

★   Scottish Rural Property & Business Association

★   Ms. Kirsten Holm Svendsen, Agriculture Counsellor, Danish Permanent Representation to the EU

Tenant Farmers Association

Mr. Kenneth Thomson, Professor Emeritus, University of Aberdeen

Ulster Farmers' Union

★   Waitrose

Wildlife and Countryside Link

Woodland Trust

APPENDIX 3: CALL FOR EVIDENCE

Introduction

The House of Lords European Union Committee will be conducting an Inquiry, via its Environment and Agriculture Sub-Committee (Sub-Committee D), into the future policy direction of the Common Agricultural Policy (CAP).

The Inquiry has been motivated by two EU-level policy initiatives. First, it has been agreed that the 2003 Reform of the CAP (Council Regulation 1782/2003 of 29 September 2003 and its implementing Regulations) will be subject to a "Health Check" in 2008. Second, the European Council decided, when adopting the 2007–13 Financial Perspectives in December 2005, that the Commission should undertake a full budgetary review to be published in 2008/9 (Council document 15915/05). Within that review, one of the specific aspects of EU spending to be addressed is the CAP.

The European Commissioner for Agriculture and Rural Development, Mariann Fischer Boel, has referred consistently in recent months to these policy initiatives as representing "one vision, two steps", in which the 2008 Health Check will involve an "adjustment" of the current situation while the budgetary review will focus on the shape of the CAP post-2013.

The purpose of the Committee's inquiry is to assess the progress thus far of the 2003 reform and to consider whether, and if so what, policy changes at the EU level are needed in both the short and the longer term. In the light of the evidence taken, the Committee aims to produce a report which will respond to the Commission's forthcoming Communication on the Health Check and at the same time provides an input into the debate over the longer-term direction of the CAP within the context of the budgetary review.

The issues

Against this background, the Committee hereby invites you to submit written evidence to the Inquiry. The Committee would find it helpful if, in addition to any general issues you may wish to raise, you would focus on a number of specific issues. It is recognised that those submitting evidence will not necessarily have an interest in all the questions and may therefore wish to be selective. The issues are:

Overview

1.   What should be the long term objectives of the CAP? Does the title "Common Agricultural Policy" aptly fit your perceived objectives of the policy? What do you consider to be the main pressures on the CAP as it currently is?

The Reformed CAP

2.   What has been your experience so far with the reformed CAP? What has worked well and less well? And where can lessons be learned?

The Single Payment Scheme

3.   Do you consider the Single Payment Scheme to be a good basis for the future of EU agricultural policy? What changes might be made at the EU level to the Single Payment Scheme, including to the rules governing entitlements, in the short and/or the longer-term?

Market Mechanisms

4.   What short and longer-term changes are required to the CAP's market mechanisms? Suggestions made by the Commission have included re-examination of certain quotas, intervention, set-aside, export refunds and private storage payments.

Rural Development

5.   What is your view on the introduction of the European Agricultural Fund for Rural Development (EAFRD)? Do you consider that it is meeting its objectives thus far? Is it suitably "strategic" in nature, meeting the needs of rural society as a whole rather than being restricted to aiding the agricultural industry? How well is it being co-ordinated with other EU and national policies on regional and rural development?

6.   Is there a case for a higher level of EU financing of rural development? Do you have a view on the extension of compulsory modulation from Pillar I (Direct Payments) to Pillar II (Rural Development)?

World Trade

7.   What benefits can the EU's World Trade Organisation obligations create for EU agriculture and, consequently, for the EU economy as a whole?

Environmental Protection and Climate Change

8.   To what extent has the system of cross-compliance contributed to an improved level of environmental protection? How is it linking with other EU policy requirements such as the Water Framework Directive?

9.   How can the CAP contribute to mitigation of, and adaptation to, climate change? What do you consider the role of biofuels to be in this regard?

Financing

10.   The Commissioner has expressed her dissatisfaction at the financing agreement reached by the Member States at the December 2005 Council. Do you consider the current budget to be sufficient? Do you consider co-financing to be a possible way forward in financing the Common Agricultural Policy?

Enlargement

11.   What has been the impact on the CAP of the 2004 and 2007 enlargements and what is the likely impact of future enlargements of the EU on the post-2013 CAP?

Simplification of the CAP and Other Issues

12.   How could the CAP be further simplified and in what other ways would you like to see the Common Agricultural Policy changed in the short and/or the long term?

APPENDIX 4: NOTE OF A MEETING WITH THE SCOTTISH EXECUTIVE

JANUARY 9 2008

Present

Brookeborough, V

Cameron of Dillington, L

Sewel, L (Chairman)

Ullswater, V

Witnesses: RICHARD LOCHHEAD, Scottish Cabinet Secretary for Rural Affairs; PETER RUSSELL, Rural Director, Scottish Executive; CORNILIUS CHIKWAMA, Economic Adviser—Agriculture, Scottish Executive; and DR ROSI WATERHOUSE, Head of CAP Reform and Crop Policy, Scottish Executive.

1.   **Lord Cameron of Dillington:** Noted that the Health Check is designed to review the implementation and effectiveness of the 2003 CAP reforms. Asked how Scotland had put those reforms into practice, and what their impact had been.

Mr Lochhead:

- Stated that he was very keen to ensure that Scotland's voice is heard.

- Mentioned that the Scottish Government is about to embark on a series of meetings with industry on this subject.

- Suggested that the 2003 CAP reforms are viewed as having been implemented quite effectively in Scotland, and that Scottish rural interests are content with the historical basis adopted for the allocation of Single Farm Payments.

- Noted that there were some small issues about access still to be dealt with.

2.   **Lord Cameron of Dillington:** Noted that Scotland has chosen to allocate Single Farm Payments on an historic basis. Asked whether the Scottish Executive welcomes the suggestion in the Commission's Communication that there should be moves towards a 'flatter' system of payment, and if so, what such a system might look like in Scotland.

Mr Lochhead:

- Noted that this proposal causes anxiety in terms of how quickly such a change might be implemented, but recognized that there will come a time when 2002—the approximate reference period for the allocation of Single Farm Payments—is a long time away, and it would therefore perhaps not be sensible to keep allocating payments on this basis.

- Stressed that the transition would be important, and that it would take time to get there, not least because Scotland's geography and topography are very disparate, so that a flat-rate payment would be unpopular and difficult to justify. Any solution would thus have to take these factors into account.

3.   **Lord Cameron of Dillington:** Asked whether the Scottish Executive envisaged introducing any reform in this regard before 2013.

Mr Lochhead:

- Stated that the Scottish Government's preference is for reform later rather than sooner.

- Pointed out that the language in the Health Check Communication is permissive, and that the Scottish Government would like to keep it that way, with no element of compulsion.

4.   **Viscount Ullswater:** Asked whether if keeping the current system until 2013 won't mean introducing a really big change after that date, rather than phasing it in slowly.

Mr Lochhead:

- Accepted that this was a fair comment, and suggested that he will have to try and think about how Scotland might get there. This is an issue that needs to be discussed with industry.

5.   **Viscount Ullswater:** Asked whether, if funds are moved from Pillar 1 to Pillar 2, this would make it more difficult to implement any change.

Mr Lochhead:

- Stressed that he would not want to introduce two massive changes at the same time.

6.   **Lord Cameron of Dillington:** Asked whether there isn't a danger that rural development cannot by carried out by farms alone, and that therefore more money is needed in Pillar 2.

Mr Lochhead:

- Suggested that it was fair to say that we are already quite far along the road of changing the emphasis of the CAP.

- Pointed out that Scotland's proposed Rural Development Programme is radically different, with a much bigger budget (£1.6 billion over 7 years). Added that the Scottish Government's contribution will be 70 per cent, higher than elsewhere, and that this was a sign of its commitment to rural development.

- Concluded that there is already a huge emphasis on rural development.

- Mentioned that farmers now say that there is too much money going into rural development, but pointed out that they too can apply for rural development funding, so that money is not being taken away from them.

7.   **Viscount Brookeborough:** Noted that European funds are rarely taken up in their entirety, and asked whether the Scottish Executive was placing an emphasis on this.

Mr Lochhead:

- Accepted that under-spending was a challenge.

- Pointed out that the Scottish Government was changing the way in which it would deliver schemes. It is introducing a system of regional priorities.

- Explained that the schemes that were oversubscribed last time around were agri-environment schemes. This time, pre-application advice will be available, so that applicants can check whether they are likely to qualify for assistance and don't waste time. In consultation with a government advisor, applicants will be able to choose among schemes, and a tailor-made package can be put together for them.

8.   **Lord Cameron of Dillington:** Asked about the diversification of Scottish farming businesses, and whether the planning system ever posed obstacles to this.

Mr Lochhead:

- Responded that farmers in Scotland have been very successful at diversifying, such as into biogas and farm shops.

9.   **Lord Cameron:** Asked how the Less Favoured Areas scheme works.

Mr Lochhead:

- Noted that one of the distinctive messages the Scottish Government wants to get across with respect to the Health Check is the ongoing need for support for Less Favoured Areas. Such support delivers social benefits and wider public benefits, and is thus not just about food production.

- Stressed that the Scottish Government was fighting to maintain that kind of support, and hoping to promote links to environmental benefits. Explained that it was under pressure from the EU to show that environmental benefits could be secured in this way.

10.   **Lord Cameron of Dillington:** Asked whether LEADER projects are also carried out on a regional basis.

Peter Russell:

- Explained that these are carried out by LEADER action groups, and that there is a single payment agency for the whole of Scotland.

11.   **Viscount Ullswater:** Asked whether there had been any problems with the implementation of cross compliance.

Peter Russell:

- Noted that there is always some low-level rumbling, but that there has been no huge outcry. On the whole, the Health Check is seen as taking cross-compliance in the right direction by addressing, among other things, disproportionate penalties—e.g. for mistakes when completing forms.

12.   **Viscount Ullswater:** Asked whether cross compliance was delivering the intended environmental benefits?

Peter Russell:

- Responded that from the Scottish Government's perspective, it was doing so.

Mr Lochhead:

- Added that cross compliance was extremely popular with NGOs, who have put a lot of effort into measuring its benefits.

13.   **Viscount Ullswater:** Asked whether the witnesses could say more about the concept of Land Management Contracts, and the respects in which they have been more and less successful.

Peter Russell:

- Explained that they are now called Rural Development Contracts. Whereas previously, separate schemes were available, the Scottish Government is now trying to offer a single framework that is as open-ended as possible.

- Stressed that the term 'contract' is not accidental, and that there is no question of an entitlement. Instead, the idea is to invite proposals. The Scottish Government will then enter into a contract with the bidder if their proposal provides them with more public benefits than alternative, competing proposals.

14.   **Lord Cameron of Dillington:** Asked how this might be measured.

Mr Lochhead:

- Suggested that the administration had sought to learn lessons from the schemes previously in place. After one year, budgets can be changed if a particular scheme has proved too popular.

15.   **Viscount Ullswater:** Asked whether the Scottish Executive views these Rural Development Contracts as a substitute for Pillar 1 in the long term?

Mr Lochhead:

- Replied that it does not.

16.   **Lord Cameron of Dillington:** Asked how Rural Development Contracts are funded.

Mr Lochhead:

- Explained that 70 per cent of funding came from the Scottish Government, 6 per cent from the EU, and the rest from voluntary modulation.

17.   **Viscount Brookeborough:** Asked whether the 70 per cent figure was ring-fenced?

Mr Lochhead:

- Explained that is committed as part of the overall spending review, and is thus ring-fenced as far as the overall rural development programme is.

18.   **Viscount Ullswater:** Drew attention to the Commission's proposals to end all sorts of 'partial' coupling so that aids meet WTO rules, and asked how Scotland was planning to deal with this, referring specifically to its Beef Calf Scheme.

Mr Lochhead:

- Explained that he agrees that legacy schemes should end, but stressed that some kind of flexibility for coupling is something the Scottish Government would like to retain. It wishes to protect at least part of the livestock, and in particular the beef sector, and doesn't want to see that sector—or the associated processing industry—disappear.

- Suggested that national envelopes might provide a way of securing these aims and therefore supported the proposal in the Health Check that the system of national envelopes be continued.

19.   **Viscount Ullswater:** Asked whether Pillar 2 might allow Scotland to continue to protect its livestock sector.

Mr Lochhead:

- Stressed that Pillar 1 is important in giving confidence to livestock producers.

- Noted that sheep have been disappearing, and that this has prompted concern over declining livestock numbers.

- Noted that he is keen to explore how Scotland can retain some flexibility to protect these sectors under Pillar 1.

- Suggested that the pendulum of opinion was now swinging back, as a consequence of the realization that with decoupling, some sectors could be more fragile than had been anticipated.

Peter Russell:

- Stressed that cattle grazing preserves the Scottish landscape, and that it was a question of whether capital can be made out of that, the answer to which was yes, by producing quality beef.

- Recognized that Scotland couldn't win a head-on battle with Argentine or Brazilian beef, but that is could preserve its market niche for high-quality produce.

20.   **Lord Cameron:** Pointed out that on most measures, quality of life in rural Scotland is infinitely better than in urban areas, and asked how this might develop in the long term.

Mr Lochhead:

- Suggested that agriculture plays a vital role in Scotland, and not just rural Scotland. The Scottish Government wants to protect that, and promote the notion of farmers as food producers, so that Scotland is well placed to benefit from future changes in food supply.

- Identified a number of challenges for the future. A first set of challenges are short-term issues that can sap confidence, such as disease, or concerns over anti-competitive practices in the food chain. A second challenge is the age profile of the sector. On paper, the opportunities for young people are few, but Mr Lochhead stressed that he had met more young people than the statistics would tell you were there in the farming sectors. He drew attention to the new entrants scheme that formed part of Scotland's rural development programme.

- Among other challenges, he cited market returns for products, while noting that some farmers were doing very well in this respect at the moment.

21.   **Viscount Brookeborough:** Asked about the Commission's proposal to end compulsory set-aside and phase out milk quotas, and whether these changes would be welcomed in Scotland.

Mr Lochhead:

- Welcomed the relaxation of set-aside, while noting that its environmental benefits might be lost.

- Also welcomed the phasing out of milk quotas, which have outlived their usefulness. Added that dairy farmers were on the whole of the same opinion.

22.   **Lord Sewel:** Asked how Scottish agriculture might adapt to, and help address the challenges posed by climate change.

Mr Lochhead:

- Emphasised that there is a lot more work to be done on this, and that the agriculture sector needed to be brought into the climate change debate.

- Noted that Scotland's Rural Development Programme includes support for renewable energy, including biomass and biogas projects. From the energy side, there is thus rising interest.

- As regards forestry, he explained that the Scottish Government wants to take forestry cover to 25 per cent, up from 17 per cent.

- With respect to soil use, he noted that carbon is wrapped up in soils, and that land use in Scotland is the second biggest sector in accounting for carbon emissions.

23.   **Lord Sewel:** Asked whether the Scottish Executive envisaged Pillar 1 funding remaining at the same level, or was anticipating a progressive transfer of funds to Pillar 2.

Mr Lochhead:

- Noted that the administration saw benefits in increasing the level of funding for Pillar 2, but given Scottish circumstances, want Pillar 1 to continue to provide support in the short- to medium-term.

24.   **Lord Sewel:** Pointed out that there were pressures on the CAP budget, and that it might thus be expected to fall over time, raising the issue of where cuts were going to come from.

Mr Lochhead:

- Recognized that it was inevitable that the funding available under Pillar 1 would decrease over time, but emphasized that the Scottish Government's concern was over the pace at which that happens.

25.   **Lord Sewel:** Asked whether there were any aspects of the Lisbon Treaty relating to agriculture, fisheries or the environment that posed particular concerns for the Scottish Executive, or that it particularly welcomed.

Mr Lochhead:

- Explained that the Scottish Government had not really debated this issue.

Peter Russell:

- Argued with respect to co-decision that the relevant changes were a strong motivation to get the Health Check sorted before they come into effect.

26.   **Lord Sewel:** Asked about the Farm Business Development Scheme.

Mr Lochhead:

- Explained that the scheme was being continued.

Peter Russell:

- Pointed out that the separateness of the scheme had been done away with, and that it is now part of the Rural Development Contracts. Noted that the old scheme was considered to have been successful and had led to some very innovative developments in areas such as tourism, and local, healthy food.

27.   **Lord Cameron:** Enquired about the percentage of rural development funding that the witnesses envisaged going into on-farm activity.

Mr Lochhead:

- Suggested that this would depend on the energy and imagination shown by farmers themselves. Explained that farmers were being asked to see themselves as part of a bigger picture. They could apply for support for land-management activities only, but were being encouraged to take a wider, more ambitious perspective and consider doing other things too.

Peter Russell:

- Added that the Scottish Government was hoping to encourage more collaboration and integration, for example with respect to flood risk management.

28.   **Lord Sewel:** Asked how support could be made available to people living in council houses—in other words, the off-farm component of rural development.

Mr Lochhead:

- Suggested that regional priorities were expected to reflect the government's national priorities, such as climate change, the promotion of local food, etc. and that increasingly addressing these issues would deliver off-farm benefits.

Mr Chikwama:

- Pointed out that Scotland had placed a particular emphasis on Axis 3 of the EAFRD, and thus on addressing social objectives in rural areas.

29.   **Lord Sewel:** Asked what the witnesses would make of the proposal to keep only a minimalist Pillar 1, and to move everything else into Pillar 2, where more imaginative and comprehensive projects could be supported.

Mr Lochhead:

- Suggested that the crux of the debate was to address the concerns of those who question why money needs to be taken away from land managers and food producers in order to achieve these wider goals.

APPENDIX 5: NOTE OF A MEETING WITH MR JOHN SCOTT MSP, MR MIKE RUMBLES MSP AND MS SARAH BOYACK MSP

JANUARY 9 2008

Present

Brookeborough, V

Cameron of Dillington, L

Sewel, L (Chairman)

Ullswater, V

Witnesses: JOHN SCOTT, Scottish Conservative Party Spokesperson on Rural Development; MIKE RUMBLES, Scottish Liberal Democrats Spokesperson on Rural Development; SARAH BOYACK, Scottish Labour Party Spokesperson on Rural Development.

1.   **Lord Sewel:** Asked how the witnesses expected the CAP to develop over the next 10 years or so, and what the impact of the 2003 CAP reforms had been on Scottish agriculture and the Scottish rural economy.

Ms Boyack:

- Stated that while environmental organisations were looking to the future of the CAP with enthusiastic expectations, there was nervousness on the part of the farming community.

- Explained that from the perspective of the Labour Party, the most important issue would be how the transition process is managed.

- The CAP should thus evolve to support communities while also securing public goods and promoting the local procurement of food (within the limits of EU procurement policy).

- Drew attention to the importance of secure food supplies, and suggested that there was huge support for sourcing fresh, and where possible, local food.

- Anticipated that in future there would be less production support.

Mr Scott:

- Noted that the 2003 reforms had been largely beneficial, and had allowed people to seek market solutions while support was still in place.

- Indicated that it would be essential that such support remains in place in Scotland, where 85 per cent of agricultural land has "less favoured area" status, as returns in the marketplace are only now returning to what they were pre-1986.

- Suggested that without that support, agricultural production in Scotland as we've known it for the last 55 years would cease.

Mr Rumbles:

- Described the 2003 reforms as positive and beneficial, having delivered benefits across the board.

- Noted that it had been right to allocate Single Farm Payments on an historic basis at the time, but that this would have to be changed if it were to avoid giving rise to anomalies. A fair transitional system would need to be applied during such a change.

- Considered it right that support should be moving from Pillar 1 to Pillar 2, but deemed it important that support should be maintained in the Highlands and Islands as those regions are special cases.

- Pointed out that the Scottish rural development budget was decreasing by 6.5 per cent over 3 years, and expressed concern that increases in voluntary modulation were being used to make up the difference.

- Stressed that his party did not have a problem with compulsory modulation, however, and that it should be increased.

2.   **Lord Sewel:** Asked to what extent the Scottish administration shared Mr Rumble's views on modulation.

Mr Rumbles:

- Indicated that he didn't think it did. Noted that Mr Lochhead was responsible for the increase in voluntary modulation.

3.   **Lord Sewel:** Summarized the responses, asking the witnesses to confirm that the reforms had been broadly welcomed, and that they saw a need to maintain support under Pillar 1, while also recognizing the necessity of increasing the resources available under Pillar 2.

Ms Boyack:

- Pointed out that she disagreed with Mike, and that Labour would have gone further with voluntary modulation, as the party does not view farming as the only industry in the rural sector.

- Emphasised that more expenditure was needed in Pillar 2, including more support for environmental measures.

Mr Scott:

- Noted that if the money taken away from farmers through modulation were given back to them, they wouldn't have a problem with it. It is when the money is allocated to others and they see their standard of living fall further that they oppose voluntary modulation.

- If there were a level playing-field in terms of modulation across Europe, farmers would support the mechanism, he suggested.

Mr Rumbles:

- Stressed that the Scottish Executive had cut its contribution to the rural affairs budget by 6.5 per cent, and compensated for it with voluntary modulation.

4.   **Lord Cameron of Dillington:** Put it to the witnesses that if one were to start again with the social and economic regeneration of the countryside, one would not start with the CAP.

Mr Scott:

- Insisted that that nobody was opposed to the objectives of Pillar 2, but to where the money comes from.

5.   **Lord Sewel:** Suggested that there appeared to be a tendency to conflate the rural and the agricultural agendas, when these were in fact different.

Mr Rumbles:

- Stressed that it was nevertheless important not to forget that especially in more remote rural areas, for example in traditional crofting communities, we don't want traditional ways of life turned around. It would have to be a mixture of the two, not all one way.

6.   **Lord Sewel:** Pointed out that a Pound could only be spent once.

Ms Boyack:

- Noted that it's important to ask what the added value of each pound spent is. Emphasised that her party would be very keen to see more rural development funding, because preserving, say, 4 jobs in a rural community would have many more knock-on effects than preserving the same number of jobs in Edinburgh Central (her constituency).

Mr Rumbles:

- Highlighted the extra transportation costs faced by farmers in Orkney, Shetland and the rest of the Highlands and Islands and that there is therefore certainly a need for some sort of agricultural support to compensate for those extra costs.

Mr Scott:

- Suggested that it was the gold-plating of red tape (regulation) that makes certain rural activities unviable.

7.   **Viscount Ullswater:** Asked the witnesses how they viewed villages in Scotland—whether populations appeared to be increasing or decreasing, and what the trends were with respect to the value of housing.

Mr Rumbles:

- Pointed out that the Rural Affairs Committee of the Scottish Parliament was launching an inquiry into rural housing, and that there was real concern that people were being driven out of homes (due to affordability issues). He noted by way of example that 50 per cent of houses in Braemar (in his own constituency) are holiday homes.

Mr Scott:

- Explained that whereas in the past, desertification payments focused on keeping people in the hills and glens, this was no longer an issue. People now do want to buy remote cottages and travel long distances and work from home. The issue now is thus instead what the land is used for, if agriculture is no more viable than in the past.

Mr Rumbles:

- Cautioned against falling into the trap of looking at Scotland as a whole. Rural Aberdeenshire and rural Highlands and Islands face different problems. Explained that in his Aberdeenshire constituency, the population was rising, and there was pressure on housing.

8.   **Lord Cameron of Dillington:** Pointed out that both remote and near countryside appeared to achieve better outcomes on most indicators than did urban areas in Scotland.

Ms Boyack:

- Noted that some work had been done on accessible rural communities last year, and it had been found that there was much less activity on the land than there used to be.

- Pointed out, however, that if climate change resulted in even small increases in temperature, this would dry out peat and increase emissions. Because of this challenge, her party was keen on more rural development.

9.   **Lord Sewel:** Suggested that wet peatlands were a public good and might thus need some support, but that rural areas in general were doing well.

Mr Scott:

- Agreed that there were great needs in urban areas too.

10.   **Lord Sewel:** Asked the witnesses where they stood on the abolition of milk quotas and set-aside.

Mr Scott:

- Explained that he did not have much to say on milk quotas, which had become valueless.

Ms Boyack:

- Suggested that thought should be given to how to preserve the environmental benefits of set-aside and that the consequences of its abolishment should be thought through to ensure that none of these were unintended.

Mr Scott:

- Added that the loss of set-aside is about setting priorities for land use, and that it is consequently right and proper that it should be abolished.

- Like Ms Boyack, however, he did not want to see its environmental benefits lost.

11.   **Lord Cameron of Dillington:** Suggested that one of the few justifications for the SFP was that it may be an 'environmental contract in-waiting'. Asked the witnesses about the extent to which we could be using cross-compliance more.

Mr Rumbles:

- Suggested that any such moves would have to be part of the Land Management Contracts in use in Scotland.

- Cross compliance at the level set now should be regarded as a minimum.

Mr Scott:

- Felt that cross compliance was encouraging travel in the right direction, but expressed concern about the red tape that came with it and the disproportionate penalties associated with the regime.

Ms Boyack:

- Suggested that cross compliance had raised the bar, and that it could be used to secure other public goods, such as biodiversity. Farmers needed to be incentivised to adopt farming practices that create habitats.

12.   **Lord Sewel:** Asked whether all this could be included Rural Development Contracts.

Ms Boyack:

- Suggested that it was to early to say how those contracts were working, but that they had been designed intelligently, with a menu of options.

- Felt that more articulation with climate change issues was necessary as climate change is a key priority for Scotland, and that more incentives for appropriate activities and behaviour needed to be provided.

13.   **Lord Sewel:** Noted that agriculture emissions were contributing to climate change, but that the sector was also in a position to make a contribution society's adaptation to it. Asked what the government could do to promote such a contribution.

Ms Boyack:

- Suggested that Rural Development Contracts would create incentives.

- She identified several areas where agriculture could make a contribution, listing among others flood management, forestry, biomass (including supply chains—not just biomass boilers), wind farms and a sensible approach to biofuels, as well as food security.

- Pointed out that advice to the farming community would be important, for example if a given area was expected to suffer more droughts.

14.   **Lord Cameron of Dillington:** Asked what capacity there was for R&D into these issues.

Ms Boyack:

- Noted that Scotland has the Macaulay Institute as well as the Scottish Agricultural Research College.

Mr Scott:

- Suggested that researchers would look at anything provided that they are funded.

- Added that climate change would necessitate that more of Scotland's land be used for food production.

- Noted that while he agreed with the proposed increase in forestry, it was not the answer, as land would come under pressure, with competing uses for it, such as public access, tourism and flood management.

- Added that tourism is by far Scotland's biggest industry, and much of it is linked to scenery—a public benefit that is delivered by Scottish land managers.

Mr Rumbles:

- Noted that the key to improving the competitiveness of Scotland's agriculture would be market forces, with the proviso that the most vulnerable communities were protected.

Ms Boyack:

- Stressed that there was no need to see forests in opposition to tourism issues, and that it was important to look for opportunities rather than viewing everything as a threat.

15.   **Lord Sewel:** Asked what one thing the witnesses would say to the Agriculture Commissioner if they had the opportunity.

Mr Rumbles:

- Said he would ask her to get rid of voluntary modulation and increase compulsory modulation.

Mr Scott:

- Said he would tell her to wake up and smell the coffee about food security and consider how, in a globally warmed world, Europe would be able to feed itself and others who can no longer produce.

Ms Boyack:

- Said she would urge her to focus on where we want to be in five to ten years' time rather than fighting the battles of the past.

APPENDIX 6: RECENT REPORTS

Recent Reports from the Select Committee

Session 2006–07

Evidence from the Minister for Europe on the Outcome of the December European Council (4th Report, Session 2006–07, HL Paper 31)

Government Responses: Session 2004–05 (6th Report, Session 2006–07, HL Paper 38)

The Commission's 2007 Legislative and Work Programme (7th Report, Session 2006–07, HL Paper 42)

Evidence from the Ambassador of the Federal Republic of Germany on the German Presidency (10th Report, Session 2006–07, HL Paper 56)

The Commission's Annual Policy Strategy for 2008 (23rd Report, Session 2006–07, HL Paper 123)

The Further Enlargement of the EU: follow-up Report (24th Report, Session 2006–07, HL Paper 125)

Evidence from the Minister for Europe on the June European Union Council and the 2007 Inter-Governmental Conference (28th Report, Session 2006–07, HL Paper 142)

Evidence from the Ambassador of Portugal on the Priorities of the Portuguese Presidency (29th report, Session 2006–07, HL Paper 143)

The EU Reform Treaty: work in progress (35th Report, Session 2006–07, HL Paper 180)

Annual Report 2007 (36th Report, Session 2006–07, HL Paper 181)

Remaining Government Responses, Session 2004–05, (37th Report, Session 2006–07, HL Paper 182)

Correspondence with Ministers (40th Report, Session 2006–07, HL Paper 187)

Recent Reports prepared by Sub-Committee D (Environment and Agriculture)

Session 2006–2007

Water Framework Directive: Making It Work (27th Report Session 2006–2007, HL Paper 136)

European Wine: A Better Deal for All (30th Report Session 2006–2007, HL Paper 144)

European Wine: A Better Deal for All Final report with evidence (39th Report, Session 2006–2007, HL Paper 184)

Session 2005–2006

The Future Financing of the Common Agricultural Policy (2nd Report Session 2005–06, HL Paper 7)

European Union Fisheries Legislation (7th Report Session 2005–06, HL Paper 24)

The United Kingdom Presidency: Defra's Priorities, (12th Report Session 2005–06, HL Paper 36)

Too much or too little? Changes to the EU Sugar Regime (18th Report Session 2005–06, HL Paper 80-I and 80-II)

Managing nuclear safety and waste: the role of the EU (37th Report Session 2005–06, HL Paper 211-I and 211-II)

The EU Strategy on Biofuels: from field to fuel (47th Report Session 2005–2006, HL Paper 267-I and 267-II)

ISBN 978-0-10-401234-5

9 780104 012345

Printed in the United Kingdom by The Stationery Office Limited
3/2008   392938   19585